B.L.E.N.D.

Building Love & Embracing a New Direction

*Mixing Well in
Your Blended Family*

LATARISS PAYNE

Thoughts & Theory Publishing, LLC

B.L.E.N.D. Building Love & Embracing a New Direction
Mixing Well in Your Blended Family
By Latariss Payne
Thoughts & Theory Publishing, LLC

Published by Thoughts & Theory Publishing, LLC O'Fallon, MO
Copyright ©2025 Latariss Payne
All rights reserved.

No part of this publication may be reproduced, stored in a retrieval system, or transmitted in any form or by any means, electronic, mechanical, photocopying, recording, scanning, or otherwise, except as permitted under Section 107 or 108 of the 1976 United States Copyright Act, without the prior written permission of the Publisher. Requests to the Publisher for permission should be addressed to Permissions Department, Thoughts & Theory Publishing, LLC, info@pathsetters.com.

Limit of Liability/Disclaimer of Warranty: While the publisher and author have used their best efforts in preparing this book, they make no representations or warranties with respect to the accuracy or completeness of the contents of this book and specifically disclaim any implied warranties of merchantability or fitness for a particular purpose. No warranty may be created or extended by sales representatives or written sales materials. The advice and strategies contained herein may not be suitable for your situation. You should consult with a professional where appropriate. Neither the publisher nor author shall be liable for any loss of profit or any other commercial damages, including but not limited to special, incidental, consequential, or other damages.

Editing and Book Design: Davis Creative, LLC, dba: DavisCreativePublishing.com

Publisher's Cataloging-in-Publication
Names: Payne, Latariss, author.

Title: B.L.E.N.D. : building love & embracing a new direction : mixing well in your blended family / Latariss Payne.

Other titles: BLEND | Building love & embracing a new direction

Description: O'Fallon, MO : Thoughts & Theory Publishing, LLC, [2025]

Identifiers: ISBN: 978-0-9993063-4-5 (paperback) | 978-0-9993063-5-2 (ebook) | LCCN: 2025900312

Subjects: LCSH: Payne, Latariss--Family. | Stepfamilies. | Stepparents--Family relationships. | Parenting. | Parent and child. | BISAC: FAMILY & RELATIONSHIPS / General. | FAMILY & RELATIONSHIPS / Parenting / Single Parent. | FAMILY & RELATIONSHIPS / Parenting / General.

Classification: LCC: HQ759.92 .P39 2025 | DDC: 306.8747--dc23

ACKNOWLEDGEMENTS

♥ **TO MY HUSBAND, CALVIN:** We married later in life, yet it feels like we've been together forever as the years have passed so quickly. Your love and commitment to our marriage and family have fulfilled and exceeded my expectations for what life could be like after we said, "I do." Doing life together as a blended family has brought me so much joy, making this journey with you a gift I treasure deeply. You have encouraged and validated me, even when you didn't realize how much I needed it, and your unwavering belief in me inspires me to grow and dream bigger. Thank you for supporting my heart's desire to write this book to help other blended families experience the kind of love and connection we are building every day.

♥ **TO OUR CHILDREN, KAYLA, CORTEZ, CAIRO, AND CALVIN III:** We couldn't have handpicked a better group of special individuals to call "our" children. We want you to know how deeply we love and appreciate each of you. Your willingness to open your hearts and minds to the idea of us becoming a close-knit family means more to us than words can express. Each of you brings unique gifts and perspectives that enrich our lives and help create a bond we value and need. Together, we can build a legacy of love, understanding, and strength that can impact us, our beautiful grandkids, and future generations. Thank you for trusting us and being an essential part of this journey—we are proud to call you our family.

NOTE FROM THE AUTHOR'S HUSBAND

LATARISS, I am so incredibly proud of the dedication and perseverance you've shown in writing this book. Every word reflects your expertise and heart, which truly cares about helping others. You have a gift for bringing hope and wisdom to both blended and traditional families, offering guidance from which so many will benefit. Watching you work tirelessly, driven by compassion and faith, has been inspiring. This book isn't just a project; it's a testament to who you are and the love you share with the world. I am blessed to stand beside you on this journey and to cheer you on every step of the way.

Love you endlessly,
Calvin Payne Jr.

CONTENTS

Foreword ix

A Poem to My Family 1

Introduction: A Recipe for Success 3

1. Before the Two Become One 11

2. Dealing with Emotional Adjustments 23

3. Building Trust and Relationships 39

4. Managing Different Parenting Styles 55

5. Co-Parenting and Coping with Ex-Partners ... 73

6. Adulting: They May Be Grown,
   But They're Not Gone 91

7. The Marriage Must Stand 103

Notes 115

FOREWORD

When I first met Latariss Payne nearly two decades ago, I had no idea how much of a blessing our friendship would become. Over the years, our bond has deepened through countless moments of laughter, tears, prayer, and celebration. Our journey together has been a testament to the power of faith, friendship, and resilience. So, it is both an honor and a joy to write the foreword for this remarkable book, *B.L.E.N.D.: Building Love and Embracing a New Direction.*

Latariss' story is more than one of navigating the complexities of a blended family; it is a blueprint for building love, trust, and connection in the face of life's greatest challenges. As someone who has walked closely with her through many of the milestones in her journey—from single parenthood to dating and ultimately to blending her family with her husband Calvin—I can attest to her authenticity, strength, and unwavering faith. She doesn't just speak about the challenges of blending families; she lives them with grace and courage.

I've seen firsthand how Latariss' faith has been her anchor through life's transitions. Her determination to build a loving and nurturing environment for her family, rooted in spiritual principles, is truly inspiring. As her spiritual accountability partner, I've had the privilege of witnessing her vulnerability, her victories, and the quiet, steadfast hope she carries in her heart. It is this hope that permeates every page of this book, offering readers strategies and a deep sense of encouragement.

I can relate to much of what Latariss shares in these pages because I, too, have walked the path of a blended family. As a teen mom who married my husband over three decades ago, I've navigated the complexities of blending families and creating a shared life. Together, my husband and I have faced challenges, embraced growth, and built a life of love, communication, and faith. It is a journey that requires patience, humility, and an open heart, all of which Latariss exemplifies so beautifully in her writing.

What makes this book so special is Latariss' ability to meet readers where they are, no matter their circumstances. She writes with the compassion of someone who understands the unique dynamics of blended families—the struggles, the triumphs, and the unexpected joys. Her words are both practical and heartfelt, offering wisdom that is as applicable to everyday life as it is to life's biggest transitions.

This book is not a set of rigid rules; it is an invitation to embrace the journey with intentionality and love. It is about finding harmony amid the chaos, building trust where there is uncertainty, and creating a legacy of love for future generations. Whether you are just starting your journey as a blended family or seeking to strengthen the bonds you've already built, *B.L.E.N.D.* will serve as a trusted guide and companion.

Latariss, thank you for pouring your heart into this book. Thank you for sharing your story so vulnerably and for giving others the courage to do the same. Your journey is a testament to God's ability to create beauty from life's most challenging circumstances. To those reading this foreword, I encourage you to dive into these pages with an open mind and a willing heart. You are holding a book that has the power to transform your family and inspire you to build something truly beautiful.

With love and admiration,
Lethia Owens, CSP
Keynote Leadership Speaker and Growth Strategist
CEO of Game Changers International, LLC

A POEM TO MY FAMILY

A New Family

As I stepped into this new chapter of life,
    I embraced the gift of becoming
    a bonus mom and wife.

Nurturing bonds with patience,
    knowing love takes time to mix just right.
Each moment we share stirs fresh memories,
    letting life take new directions, bold and bright.
When I think of family now, I see all of your faces—
    a reflection of love blended in beautiful light.

Finding joy as we navigate this recipe of
    love, trust, and grace.
As a couple, we're committed to forever savoring
    each season at a steady pace.
Mixing our hearts with unity, knowing love is the
    key to a strong foundation.
Inviting all of our children to a table where belonging
    isn't a question but an affirmation.
Letting shared experiences strengthen us, like
    ingredients that must be stirred with care.
Yielding to God's perfect plan, trusting He is crafting
    something for the next generation to share.

INTRODUCTION

A Recipe for Success

> *"Becoming a blended family means mixing, mingling, scrambling, and sometimes muddling our way through delicate family issues, complicated relationships, and individual differences, hurts, and fears."*
> —Tom Frydenger

I have a soft spot for kitchen gadgets. Whenever I spot a new item promising to cut prep time, enhance my cooking experience, or transform my kitchen into *Top Chef*, I feel that familiar rush of excitement. It's like discovering a shiny new toy, sparking visions of all the incredible dishes I'll create. But that initial warm and fuzzy sensation fades almost as quickly as it arrives, often giving way to the sober realization that, if I'm honest, I don't really love to cook.

It's not that I hate cooking—I can cook, and I do. I cook because I love to eat and because there's something deeply satisfying about feeding my family good food. However, I'd rather spend my time doing almost anything else, like cleaning my house. Baking is even lower on my list; I have no interest in crafting desserts or dishes that demand the patience of scratch preparation. I've never walked past a stand mixer or a set of elegant mixing bowls and felt a rush of adrenaline. But blenders? Blenders are a different story. They always catch my eye. I like my smoothies smooth, without any clumps or chunks to disrupt the texture. A blender that guarantees perfect consistency every time is almost too good to resist. Still, I often hesitate before I add yet another fancy kitchen widget to my cart, remembering the many gadgets I've purchased in the past that now gather dust after one or two uses.

A blended family can feel much like assembling the perfect smoothie. You mix various ingredients with unique tastes and textures until they come together into a smooth, cohesive whole. But instead of fruits and vegetables, we're combining personalities, histories, and temperaments. It takes time, trial, and error, but with the right balance, you can make a new family unit that supports everyone.

Before we dive into the nuances of the blended family, it's good to understand different family structures and clearly define the label/phrase. Traditional families, often referred to as nuclear families, are made up of two parents—a married couple—and their children. These families often include one or more biological children, with the parents working together to raise them in a shared household.[1] For those who hold traditional marriage in high regard, the two-parent structure is often seen as the ideal foundation for starting and raising a family, barring situations of abuse. Even if the marriage isn't fully supported by family or friends, it is generally considered wise for a couple to begin their family journey within the commitment of marriage. This approach leaves little room for criticism within the framework of traditional marriage values. The traditional two-parent family structure has been declining, with divorce, remarriage, and cohabitation on the rise. In some countries, non-traditional families now outnumber traditional ones.[2] For our purposes, I'll define a blended family as a husband, wife, the children they have together, and one or more children from previous relationships.[3] While there are several types of blended families, we'll use this simplified definition to cover the basics.

Blended families often come together after a marriage or dating relationship falls apart or following the loss of a spouse. When two separate families merge, traditional roles can get as tangled as a pair of wired earbuds in a pocket. Many times, we focus on the marriage and give little thought to the kids involved, optimistically assuming the children will share the adults' joy or at least go along with the plan. But in reality, the kids' reactions can fall into a confusing gray area that leaves the happy couple scratching their heads and wondering what they got themselves into. It's like expecting a refreshing fruit smoothie, only to take a sip and realize it tastes more like a watery blend of leftover veggies—not at all what you were hoping for. Mixing well in a blended family can be as tricky as stirring various ingredients into a perfect smoothie. Just as a blender struggles to evenly combine distinct textures and flavors, children and stepparents often find themselves working overtime to adjust to changes.

Now, what about me? At the tender age of forty-five, I transitioned from being a single mother of one child to a wife and mother of four—three of whom were adults, including my son, plus a teenager. Most of the time, I refer to my husband's biological children as "our" children. However, when I need to differentiate them from my son, I lovingly call them my "bonus kids." My favorite tumbler cup reads, "Best Bonus Mom Ever." The term "bonus" resonates with me because it speaks to the significant responsibility of stepping in with love and care to help raise your spouse's children. While I use both "bonus" and "step" throughout this book, "stepparent" and "stepchild" remain terms of endearment for many.

If I could rewrite my life narrative, it would undoubtedly include raising my son in a loving, two-parent home. However, by the time my son was six, his father and I had divorced, and I remained single until he was nineteen. As a single mother, I could write a book about the enormous responsibility of raising a child alone. Oh, wait, I did write that book. In *S.P.I.L.L.—Single Parents Inspiring Love and Legacy*, I share my experiences raising my son and provide practical guidance to help other single parents build strong relationships with their children: relationships that develop deep, lasting family values. My life has alternated between single-parent and blended family structures, making me a two-time participant in blended families as an adult. Before my son was born, his father already had two children. My current husband and I each brought children into our blended family. I don't see this as something to be proud or ashamed of—it's simply my story. I'm happy to say that this second marriage has been much more meaningful, thanks to personal growth, healing, and the intentional love and encouragement my husband and I show each other and our family.

My journey as a bonus mom has not been without challenges. Thankfully, in my first marriage and current family, I've been blessed with loving, authentic relationships with my bonus kids and mutual respect with their biological mothers. This has allowed us to co-parent successfully, free from significant conflicts. Fortunately, I've never had to deal with biological parents who resist my involvement or bonus kids who reject the idea of building a relationship with me. I experienced separation and divorce myself, both as a child living with my mother and later as an adult who made the same decision. My extensive experience with blended families, both personally and through others' insights, inspired me to write this book—to encourage and guide those who find themselves grappling with the complexities of blended family life. I hope to share the triumphs and the challenges I've endured to help others navigate their journeys. By openly discussing what worked, what didn't, and the lessons I learned, I hope to guide and encourage families to find their way. I want my story to inspire strength, resilience, and unity, showing that even if challenges exist, the path can lead to lasting bonds.

While I deeply value traditional biological parenting, I can't ignore that 40% of U.S. families are blended, with at least one partner bringing a child from a previous relationship into the marriage.[4] Because not all remarriages are stepcouples, the current rate of divorce for stepfamilies is not easy to determine. We have fewer studies and more inconsistent data on stepfamily divorce than any other population, so an exact number is difficult to calculate. However, based on the information from recent studies, an estimated current divorce rate of stepfamily couples is roughly 45–50%, and a projected divorce rate is roughly 50–60%.[5] These statistics are telling and, even more concerning, they don't reflect the emotional, financial, and psychological toll on parents and children who are replanted in new families and homes.

Blended families face unique challenges that are absent in marriages where both partners are raising their biological children. Building a new family requires work, and a blended family's foundation needs more than the love of the happy couple. It's essential to embrace a package deal when entering a marriage that includes minor children from previous relationships. Even if a deep connection between a stepparent and stepchild doesn't develop immediately, there must be a genuine desire to forge that union. When you say, "I do," in a blended family, you say, "I do take you, and I take your children."

It's easy to forget amid the complexities that children are innocent bystanders. They don't choose to be born, they don't choose divorce or a parent's death, and they certainly don't choose the upheaval of a blended family. Yet, they're the ones caught in the middle—their lives reshaped by decisions they had no part in making. This realization should fuel our compassion and commitment as parents and stepparents. We must strive to provide a stable, loving environment where these children entrusted to our care can thrive despite the uncertainty of their circumstances.

This book isn't a step-by-step manual for building your blended family to match a picture-perfect ideal. A family's success isn't based on a snapshot but on shared core values, commitment, and intentional efforts to create authentic connections. While it's terrific to see blended families thrive early in marriage, meaningful relationships often ripen over time. Many families have been disappointed by the unrealistic expectation that strong bonds must form immediately. In Dr. Gary Chapman's book *Building Love Together in Blended Families: The 5 Love Languages and Becoming Stepfamily Smart*, he explains that blended families encounter distinct challenges, and unfortunately, good intentions alone may not suffice. The dynamics of these families involve intricate relationships, which can alter the usual principles of family life—including how something as straightforward as the five love languages is applied.[6] This is a very profound statement, reinforcing the need to give special attention to the dynamics of blended families. In this book, I'll weave together the voices of parents and children, offering a balanced perspective to help your blended family grow stronger and find encouragement along the way.

As with my previous book, *S.P.I.L.L.—Single Parents Inspiring Love and Legacy*, my motivation for writing this narrative is to help build strong families. As a stepparent, you contribute to the legacy of love passed down to your spouse's children. Consider this book a trusted friend offering encouragement, suggestions, and practical guidelines for those preparing to marry into a blended family or those already married and wanting to strengthen their family connections. Let's gather a few practical ingredients before mixing all the family pieces together.

CHAPTER ONE

Before the Two Become One

*"Marriage doesn't create problems. It reveals them.
You bring unresolved stuff into it."*
—Rick Warren

The quote by Rick Warren is relevant to every marriage, from your first to your third, whether you're young, old, have children, or are starting fresh. It's especially true for blended families, where the intricacies of merging lives amplify unresolved baggage. The inherent challenges of uniting two families, navigating different parenting styles, and managing the emotional complexities of stepparenting magnify any pre-existing personal trauma. Unresolved issues around trust, communication, boundaries, and past relationships can resurface under the pressures of blended family life. Recognizing this truth empowers individuals to embark on a journey of self-reflection and healing before entering into such a commitment, paving the way for a healthier, more successful blended family dynamic.

Before diving into how I began to build love and embrace a new direction with my blended family, I want to offer some hard-earned wisdom to those who've navigated the challenges of divorce. While overall divorce rates are high—43% for first marriages, 67% for second, and a staggering 73% for third—these statistics aren't specific to blended families. Like any major life event, second and third marriages present both challenges and opportunities.[1] It's crucial to be fully free from your past divorce or even a cohabitation relationship before embarking on a new marriage and blended family for several reasons. Divorce, or the end of a significant relationship, often involves emotional wounds, unresolved issues, and lingering baggage. Entering a new marriage without addressing these can form a shaky foundation, leaving you vulnerable to slipping into old patterns or projecting old hurts onto your new partner and family. Taking time to heal and gain closure allows you to enter the new relationship with a clean slate and a healthier emotional state. Baggage can include emotional, financial, and legal issues you want resolved and settled before remarrying. Jealousy and insecurity are known culprits of destroying any marriage and can easily arise if you haven't fully processed and moved on from your previous experiences. Taking time for self-reflection and healing allows you to enter your new relationship with greater emotional maturity and resilience. By demonstrating that you have fully moved on from your past relationship, you can build a strong and successful blended family, one that allows you to prioritize your present marriage and build a healthy future.

Licensed psychologist Larry F. Waldman noted:

> Common sense suggests that someone who remarries is older, wiser, more mature, has learned from their mistakes, and knows better what they want and need in a partner. Therefore, the divorce rate for second marriages would be expected to be substantially lower than the rate for first marriages. Despite our common sense expectations, according to demographic data, the divorce rate for subsequent marriages is, in fact, significantly higher than that of first marriages—65%, nearly two out of three! Why?[2]

He identifies five major reasons second marriages fail at a high rate:

- Money, sex, and in-laws (top three)
- Children
- Exes
- The speed at which we re-couple
- Unconscious dynamics

I will discuss these topics throughout the book. Regardless of the circumstances, once divorce enters the picture the first time, you must work hard to not make it an option for you and your new spouse. Children deserve the healthiest version of you to change the trajectory of your blended family's future.

Freedom from Your Past Changes Your Tomorrow

I was divorced and single for over thirteen years before I met my husband, Calvin. In all that time, I never had a serious relationship, just occasional dating here and there. Despite moments of loneliness and the occasional wish for someone special, I was genuinely content. My life felt whole, and I was happy in my singleness. I was a single mother parenting an eighteen-year-old son and ready to embrace an empty-nest life. I looked forward to my son's independence and entry into adulthood even though he remained uncertain about his plans after high school. During this time, I envisioned what I wanted for the future and poured my energy into my career, volunteering, and personal goals. My life felt like it was on cruise control, and I had reached a place where "simple is better" became my guiding mantra. I was open to something different, though I hadn't anticipated that it would be a new relationship.

My story with Calvin began at a strange time: the global pandemic was here and the world felt more virtual than real. Although I was skeptical about online dating—after all, I'd tried it before and found it overwhelming, artificial, and exhausting—a friend persuaded me to give it one last shot. So, I set up a profile and kept my expectations low. But within a day, Calvin's profile popped up as a match. He was handsome, and his interests lined up surprisingly well with mine. His initial message was warm and genuine and cut through the usual small talk. After a quick exchange, we agreed that endless app messages weren't our style, so we exchanged numbers and moved our talks to the phone. Over the next few days, our chats became easy, respectful conversations. Calvin seemed as interested as I was in building a real friendship first—not just racing toward the "dating" label.

By the end of the week, we decided it was time to meet in person. We settled on a Panera Bread; a place casual enough to ease the first-meeting jitters. I arrived early, feeling slightly nervous under my cool, calm, and collected exterior. I strategically chose a seat by the window, planning a swift exit if he turned out to be anything other than the man from his pictures. Meeting someone from an app in the flesh, especially when so little felt real, made me nervous.

Would he be like the man who captured my interest during our phone conversations? Or would he be altogether different—maybe a serial online dater with hidden agendas, or worse yet, a full-blown lunatic? Calvin texted to say he'd be a few minutes late, and for a moment, I wondered if he'd show up at all. With time to kill, I checked my hair in my phone camera and gave myself a last once-over. Just as I glanced at the parking lot, I turned toward the order line—and froze. A tall, handsome man who looked even better in person came in through what must have been a side entrance. A dozen greeting options ran through my mind as he made his way over: A casual hello? A handshake? Or maybe a hug? I had no idea. But when our eyes met, the decision felt natural. Without a word, we stepped into a quick, cautious hug, warm enough to break the ice but careful enough to respect the newness of it all. I'll share more of our story as we go, but we became husband and wife exactly one year after that first meeting at Panera Bread.

Meeting Calvin during that time felt like a rare gift. He was navigating his own life as a father with an adult daughter and two sons still at home. We were our children's primary caregivers, decision-makers, and support systems. Still, given that we had both been divorced and had been stepparents before, we knew that blending two families required a different approach. Each of us brought our unique experiences and histories to the table, and our children each had distinct relationships and roles within our lives. We embarked on this journey with eyes wide open, perhaps more cautious than most. The sting of divorce and the pain of watching children navigate a fractured family fueled a fierce determination to have something lasting, something different. We understood the profound impact our choices would have on our children and the generations to come. With their fresh eyes and open hearts, my bonus grandchildren will only know a family woven together by love. They won't remember a time before their "bonus" granny, a time when we weren't a family. They will inherit a legacy of unity—a testament to the power of love and commitment to build a new and whole life together. Theirs is a heritage enriched by diverse perspectives, strengthened by resilience, and defined by our unwavering bond. This is the gift we give them: a family united, a love that surpasses biology, and a future overflowing with hope.

The weight of that responsibility was heavy and exhilarating. We did not overlook that we were resetting the course of our families, tossing our unique ingredients into the blender of life to, hopefully, form flavors of love, strength, and hope. This union wasn't just about us but about building a legacy that would ripple through our family tree and touch lives far beyond our own. Step into your new marriage with hearts ready to embrace your blended family, not with the weight of past hurts and unresolved issues. This emotional preparedness creates a ripple effect that impacts each member of your household. Your spouse feels secure in your commitment, your biological children and stepchildren witness a healthy relationship model, and you create a solid ground to build love and pave the way toward deeper individual and family connections.

Before "I Do" or "I Do" Again:
Evaluate Readiness for a Blended Family

When your potential blended family involves minor children from previous relationships, there is another level of consideration that a couple must give to their decision to marry. Couples who marry without children, whether for the first time or in later marriages, experience a unique freedom in their relationship, where their focus remains entirely on each other. Without the demands of parenting—scheduling, disciplining, and co-parenting—they are free to nurture their bond and grow together without the responsibilities of raising children. They can prioritize each other's needs, pursue shared goals, and enjoy the spontaneity that can be harder to maintain in a family centered around children. This allows them to explore their partnership fully, establishing a foundation that is often less complicated and more flexible than relationships that involve the care of children. Marriage requires effort, with or without children. Many challenges—such as serious illness, loss of a loved one, financial strain, intimacy issues, and other difficult situations—can test a couple's bond. These difficulties can complicate any relationship and require resilience and mutual support to overcome. But when stepchildren are added to the mix, it's like introducing a new ingredient to a smoothie—the entire flavor changes, creating a blend that requires even more careful balance.

Choosing to marry and create a blended family is not just about the union of two adults; it's about embracing the whole recipe, stepchildren included—especially minor children whose young hearts are being shaped by their own unique experiences. They are not optional add-ins but essential ingredients to the recipe of your future together. Couples must have honest conversations about co-parenting and stepparenting long before exchanging vows. True success in a blended family requires a complete commitment, a willingness to embrace the whole child, and a shared understanding that caring for your future spouse's child is a non-negotiable for a new stepfamily to blend well.

Premarital counseling made me well aware that a deficiency may exist for couples entering into a blended family to have honest dialogue and gain insights into practical ways to help their family thrive. When couples combine premarital counseling with family counseling, they give themselves and their children a safe space to express concerns, ask questions, and share expectations. It equips everyone with tools to manage potential conflicts, set realistic boundaries, and foster positive relationships from the start. This proactive approach can also help children feel more secure in the transition as they gain confidence that their voices and emotions are recognized and valued. Your happiness is important, but so are the lives of your children. A blended family starts with a healthy and united marriage, but it will flourish if we continue with trust, love, and consideration for how each other is growing. Before you decide to remarry, consider whether you're ready, talk to your partner about what it means, and prepare your children for what comes next.

~BLENDED FAMILIES 101~
Identifying the Needs of Your Blended Family

What practical considerations should you think about before getting married, and if you're already married, what practical things did you expect to work that aren't?

Evaluating where you will live, the impact of changing schools, parenting styles, and legal matters are just a few practical points to consider before you bring two unique families together. If you are already married, how are your decisions playing out? Couples can significantly enhance their chances of creating a fulfilling blended family life by prioritizing practical considerations and addressing potential challenges early on. Some issues you identify while dating won't disappear because you say, "I do."

What are your expectations for your blended family?

If you are blending families, especially with younger children, talking openly about everyone's roles and responsibilities is essential. Ideally, this happens before marriage, in premarital counseling, or in dedicated conversations. But even if you're already married, there's always time to clear the air, especially if there's tension. This helps uncover assumptions about everyone's roles, expectations, and how you will handle things like discipline, chores, and decision-making. It can clarify and reduce misunderstanding as your family evolves.

What are your long-term goals for your blended family, and how will you work together to achieve them?

Goals of any kind create a sense of purpose and direction, whether in business, sports, or, even more importantly, for your blended family. This could be as simple as scheduling a family night once a week, a monthly family dinner to get adult children involved, or an annual family vacation. Don't establish arbitrary goals. Be intentional in establishing goals that make sense for you and your family and promote quality time and connection.

Would you and your future spouse or current spouse benefit from professional guidance?

Even if there are no apparent problems, consider counseling, workshops, or books designed explicitly for blended families. These resources provide insights, strategies, and tools to help you strengthen your relationship and ensure a smoother transition for everyone involved. Professional guidance can also provide a safe space to reflect on advice, identify your family's unique needs, and give you an environment where each of you feels heard and valued.

CHAPTER TWO

Dealing with Emotional Adjustments

"The blended family isn't just an ordinary family, times two. It's a special kind of family with special needs"
—Maxine Marsolini

According to family therapist and author Ron Deal:

> Children who feel included in decisions related to forming a blended family and free to speak into the process find embracing the new family easier than children who aren't, and now there's evidence of that. Researchers examining the importance of involving children in blended family educational courses concluded, 'When it comes to strengthening couples in stepfamilies, the involvement of children is clearly implicated and should not be underestimated.'[1]

Think of it like blending a delicate smoothie. Younger kids might need a gentle "pulse"—short bursts of involvement where you check in, answer questions, and offer reassurance. Older kids can handle more of a "blend"—ongoing conversations and a say in decisions, such as how a new room might be decorated or deciding what activities you will do for family night as a new tradition. Either way, actively involving them in the process, at a pace that feels right for their age, helps them feel heard and less overwhelmed by the changes swirling around them.

I was twelve or thirteen when my mother decided to add a new ingredient to our family by marrying my first stepfather. She had never been married, and my brother and I came from different recipes—my brother's father had passed away when he was around four, and my father was in prison when I was born, later abandoning me after his release. We never had a father figure in our home. So, when Mom dropped the bombshell that she was getting married and we were moving, it felt like someone pressed the "blend" button on my life—and I wasn't sure what kind of smoothie was going to come out of it. It was a one-sided conversation with no preparation. All I knew was that I *really* didn't want to be poured out of the comfy container I had with Grandma, my home, and my school. My whole world was uprooted and replanted somewhere I didn't choose.

My world was abruptly tilted on its axis, and I faced the idea of a new house, a new town, and a new stepfather. Many parents in my mother's situation wouldn't have tried to understand how my brother and I felt or how the transition into our blended family could have gone smoother. I was entering the seventh grade, and the thought of moving to another state and attending a new school made me sad. Living with my grandmother was everything. Her house was familiar, warm, inviting, nurturing, and downright fun. The house was always full of people and love. My grandmother wasn't keen on me moving with my mother, and she fought the good fight to keep me in her care—and won. I would go to my mother's house every other weekend, which made a pretty cool getaway. However, the following school year, my mother demanded I live with her full-time and go to my grandmother's house every other weekend. When my mother married, as best I recall, she handled most things about me. If she ever consulted my stepfather, it must have been behind closed doors.

My stepdad came with a "bonus pack" of two sons from different moms. One was younger than me and popped up every blue moon, and the other, a year older than my brother, was around more often. Even before he and my mom got together, I knew my stepdad wasn't winning the Father of the Year award. Let's just say we never quite reached *Brady Bunch* levels of family bonding. As a teenager, I vividly recall my mother telling her ex-husband, "Don't make me choose between you and my kids." Though I was likely eavesdropping, I never forgot her words. They implied that if forced to choose, she would pick her children over her marriage. Eventually, they separated and divorced. At the time, I didn't think their failed marriage had anything to do with my brother and me. While I believe other issues contributed to their decision, my adult mind now processes that ultimatum more deeply. Though I understood what she meant, I couldn't comprehend what situations could lead to divorce after we had uprooted our lives for a fresh start just five years earlier.

When I reflect on my mother's ultimatum to my stepfather, I'm not surprised they had disagreements about how to handle specific parental situations. My mother ran a tight ship, firmly enforcing her rules, often leaving little room for my stepfather's influence. I stayed compliant, keeping my head down to avoid chaos. I wasn't one to push boundaries—I respected my mother deeply, but I also feared her enough to avoid any consequences of stepping out of line. Looking back, her parenting leaned heavily into control—focused more on obedience, responsibility, and performance than on fostering a close connection. My brother and I were both teenagers, forming our own identities and trying to fit into our stepfamily life. We rebelled in our own ways, with my brother exploding and me imploding.

With my stepdad's occasional "man of the house" power moves layered over my mom's already strict rules, adjusting to the new household dynamics was anything but a walk in the park. The first year seemed smooth, but over time, my brother and stepdad became like oil and water. And I had a few *dramatic* moments to show how much I disliked our new living situation. Believe it or not, I tried to pull off a fake runaway attempt. Spoiler alert: It backfired. Big time.

Living under the same roof didn't magically create a close-knit family. By the time my mom and stepdad split, my brother lived on his own, leaving me alone to piece together the remains of my high school years. As I neared graduation, their marriage unraveled completely, and with it, the household rules vanished. No one checked on me, and I felt invisible and uncertain of what I could say or how to feel about everything. Outwardly, I seemed fine, but inside I was numb and confused. I planned to go to college a little farther from home, but when my mother moved us out of the house, I felt an unexpected pull to stay close. Instead, I enrolled in community college and started working nearby, feeling somehow responsible for her—even though my mother was one of the strongest, most independent women I'd ever known.

Those five years felt like a lifetime, an emotional roller coaster ride I couldn't escape. When Mom married my stepfather, I was a teenager, already experiencing the hormonal turbulence of adolescence. His presence added another layer of uncertainty, a quiet unease that settled over our home. He wasn't overtly mean, but neither was he kind. It was a constant state of neutrality, a feeling of not belonging, of being an outsider in my own family. I oscillated between anger and resentment, longing for the familiar comfort of our previous life and a forced acceptance, trying to convince myself that this was my new normal. The divorce, when it finally came, sparked a strange mix of relief and grief. Relief that the tension disappeared; grief for the family I'd never truly called my own. It was a stark reminder that even seemingly subtle shifts in family dynamics can leave deep imprints on a young person's emotional landscape that shapes their sense of self and their understanding of relationships for years to come.

Supporting Each Other Through Loss

It wasn't easy to watch my mother battle to guide our blended families. Life doesn't come with a manual or a foolproof formula, especially when it involves complex relationships and significant shifts in family roles. Blended families face a unique set of challenges. Both adults and children may grapple with feelings of loss, grief, or insecurity as they learn a new family structure and the emotional strain that often arise in the wake of marriage. These emotions aren't confined to the initial blending phase; they can emerge or resurface unexpectedly, testing the bonds of the new family unit.

As my dating relationship with Calvin deepened, I yearned for a sign that we were both on the same page and heading toward a future together. Then, one weekend, he invited me to meet his mother. Knowing how close they were, I understood the significance of this gesture. It was a silent affirmation of his commitment, a clear sign of his desire for me to enter his inner circle. It felt like a green light, a silent promise of a potential future together. When I married Calvin, I gained a new extended family. I was excited to have a new mother figure in my life to build a loving bond with, to share holidays with, and to seek advice from.

But life has a way of rewriting our plans. Just a year after we said our vows, Calvin's mother passed away. Her loss left a void we weren't prepared for, plunging us into a period of grief that shook the foundations of our young marriage. Her passing triggered a sharp pang of familiarity for me; nine years earlier, I had said goodbye to my own mother, who had succumbed to cancer. That loss left its scars, and now those wounds were reopened as I watched Calvin face his own heartbreak. Suddenly, we were navigating grief together but in different ways. Calvin needed space to mourn his mother while I kept revisiting the ache of my past loss. At the same time, I felt the weight of responsibility to hold our newly formed family together. That meant offering strength to Calvin and his children while I managed my own emotions. It was a delicate dance, balancing my role as a wife, bonus mother, and grieving daughter-in-law.

There were moments when the grief felt insurmountable—when tears would flow without warning, and life seemed heavy with the absence of her presence. Yet, there were also moments of connection. I felt my bond with Calvin deepen during the beautiful times I listened to him share stories about his mother. We found solace in one another's presence, and through that shared sorrow, resilience began to grow.

This experience taught me that building a blended family isn't just about blending schedules, traditions, or homes. It's about blending emotions—recognizing that everyone comes with their own history, pain, and way of processing it. For Calvin and me, losing his mother became a crucible for our relationship. It solidified our commitment to support each other, even when we didn't have all the answers, and to find strength in moments when it felt like none existed. Blended families must be prepared to weather storms they didn't foresee. There will be grief, tension, and moments of doubt. But with love, patience, and the willingness to adapt, there's also the potential to emerge stronger and more united. The journey may be unpredictable, but it's in those twists and turns that the bonds of family are truly shaped.

From Friend to Fiancé to Spouse

Minor children in a blended family often experience a whirlwind of emotions as they watch someone transition from their biological parent's friend to a significant other and then their spouse. Initially, they may feel curiosity or excitement, but this can shift to uncertainty, fear of change, or even jealousy as the relationship becomes more serious. The permanence of marriage can bring mixed feelings, including hope for a stronger family unit, but anxiety can arise about losing their biological parent's attention or adjusting to new rules and priorities. It's essential for adults to acknowledge these emotions, provide reassurance, and cultivate good communication to help children navigate these changes and feel secure in the evolving family structure.

When Calvin and I first started dating, his youngest son, Calvin III (C3), was ten. Calvin had raised him to be respectful and kind, which was evident in every interaction. When I visited their home in those early days, C3 eagerly asked if I could stay the night. With the innocence and excitement of a child, he'd say, "Can you spend the night? We can have a sleepover!" He saw me not as an intruder into their relationship but as someone who could add joy and laughter to their lives, much like one of his dad's friends or a play buddy. It was endearing and sweet. The three of us spent evenings together, watching movies, going to his basketball games, or just hanging out. C3's youthful enthusiasm made everything more enjoyable, and I cherished those moments. As my relationship with Calvin deepened, the dynamics between C3 and me also shifted.

C3 was thrilled when Calvin and I decided to marry. He was excited to have me around as a "permanent" play buddy. Yet, as the reality of our marriage set in, those innocent sleepover requests faded away, replaced by something more complex and profound. Becoming Calvin's wife meant stepping into a new role—not just as his partner but also as a bonus mom to his son. While C3 remained the same fun-loving boy, subtle changes in our relationship emerged. The transition from "Dad's lady-friend" to "Dad's wife" introduced new expectations and boundaries. Our time together was no longer just about fun and games; it became about creating a family dynamic that honored existing bonds while building new ones.

C3 no longer asked for sleepovers; he understood that my presence in his life was now permanent. We began to address the complexities of our new family structure. There were moments of adjustment—times when C3 wasn't sure how to relate to me as a parental figure. The easy-going relationship we once shared evolved into something more refined, requiring mutual understanding and respect.

I had to balance my relationship with Calvin while also nurturing my bond with C3. I learned when to step in and when to step back, allowing C3 and his father to maintain their unique connection while also establishing my own with him. This wasn't always smooth sailing. There were times when C3 would test the boundaries of our new relationship, but with patience and love, we slowly found our rhythm. Over time, our connection deepened, with me becoming someone C3 could rely on for encouragement and guidance. The affection we developed for each other gradually grew stronger as we adjusted to our new roles within the family. I was no longer just "Dad's lady-friend"—I was his bonus mom—a constant figure in his life who loved him and cared deeply for his well-being.

As I reflect on our journey, my heart swells with compassion for our youngest son. He's navigated a labyrinth of emotions from the gradual acceptance of a new family dynamic to the loss of his grandmother to juggling different home routines and bravely facing the uncertainty of being part of a blended family. Yet, through it all, we've helped him embrace our ever-evolving family. We continue to navigate the mazes with unwavering support and a shared commitment to creating a haven where he feels safe, cherished, and truly at home. Though the path may have unexpected twists and turns, I'm confident that our love and dedication will pave the way for a future where our entire family flourishes—not despite our blended family dynamics, but because of the unique strength and resilience it has developed within us.

The transition wasn't a walk in the park, but it was a journey worth taking. As we prepared for a long-term future, I became a part of Calvin's children's lives, just as he did for my son. This enriched all of us. We've had purposeful conversations about our roles and parenting styles when handling things like day-to-day activities, discipline, and every unforeseen thing in between. We've always intended to build our relationships based on trust, respect, encouragement, and love—traits that grow stronger as we do life together. Each experience brings an opportunity for deeper connections—to strengthen our family, bring us closer together, and help us evolve.

Calvin and I had open conversations with each of our children about our decision, but unlike the deep, meaningful talks we had with each other, we didn't fully engage our kids in exploring their feelings about our marriage. This includes our adult children, who might have had valuable perspectives to share. For instance, a few years after Calvin and I married, my son admitted he had struggled with the adjustment. It was just him and me for so long that he missed my presence and needed more support than he knew how to request since we no longer lived in the same home. This experience taught me that, even for grown children, a parent's marriage can bring changes they need help navigating.

Like any good smoothie, the right combination of ingredients—patience, love, encouragement, and understanding—creates something truly special. Calvin and I didn't just gain a spouse; we gained a family, and through that process, we learned how to blend our lives together to create a new and fulfilling family structure. This process looks different for every family. Still, the base ingredients for the recipe, which are two emotionally healthy individuals, are critical to building a strong marriage and mixing well in a blended family.

~BLENDED FAMILIES 101~
How Can You Explore Feelings About the Changing Family Dynamics?

What are each family member's biggest fears or anxieties about the transition? If you are married, how does each family member feel in your specific stage of your blended family?

> Create a safe space for everyone to express their feelings and validate their emotions without judgment. Encourage open communication through family meetings, individual conversations, or journaling, allowing each person to share their concerns at their own pace. Addressing these emotions head-on reduces anxiety and promotes a sense of security during this period of change. Acknowledging and validating each other's feelings creates a stronger, more connected family unit capable of navigating challenges together.

What are some positive aspects of the new or existing blended family dynamic that you can focus on?

> Actively seek out and acknowledge the strengths within your family, such as increased support systems, diverse perspectives, and unique talents. Celebrate individual and collective achievements, reinforcing a sense of belonging and shared purpose.

Express gratitude for the new connections and relationships formed, and cultivate a culture of appreciation within the family. By focusing on the positives, you build a strong foundation for navigating challenges and building a loving and supportive family environment.

How can you celebrate each person's unique strengths and qualities in the blended family?

Celebrating each person's unique strengths and qualities promotes an environment of respect, appreciation, and unity. This can be achieved by acknowledging individual achievements, encouraging personal interests, and creating traditions where family members can showcase their talents. For example, hosting a "family spotlight night" or simply praising specific contributions during family discussions can build confidence and a sense of belonging. When everyone feels valued for who they are, it reduces resentment and promotes cooperation, as each member sees their worth in the family dynamic.

As a couple, what can you do if you discover displeasure or acting out from the children, including stepsibling rivalries?

These are concerns that can be a source of extreme stress and tension and cause animosity and frustration. Be supportive of kids' honest and open expression of emotions and assure them they will not be judged. Validate their feelings and their pains and give them clear expectations for behavior. Encourage them to empathize with one another by helping them see things from each other's point of view. Make connections by spending one-on-one time with each child to listen to their needs and worries. If issues persist or worsen, talk to a therapist or counselor trained in dealing with blended family dynamics.

CHAPTER THREE

Building Trust and Relationships

"The strength of the team is each member. The strength of each member is the team."
—Phil Jackson

Early in his career, Michael Jordan believed his talent alone could secure championships. Despite his incredible efforts and achievements, including being drafted by the Chicago Bulls in 1984 and earning Rookie of the Year in 1985, the team still struggled to reach championship success. At the time, the Bulls had a poor reputation, but Jordan's relentless drive to be the best kept him focused on the game and in the gym. By 1989, though Jordan had won the league's MVP Award, the team had yet to claim a championship. That year, Phil Jackson was promoted to head coach and introduced a new strategy called "the triangle offense," developed by assistant coach Tex Winter. Unlike traditional plays that relied heavily on a single player, typically the point guard, the triangle offense emphasized teamwork. It positioned players in a way that encouraged ball movement and collaboration, allowing anyone on the team to contribute as a playmaker.

For Jordan, this approach meant sharing the spotlight and trusting his teammates. Coach Jackson helped him understand that winning championships required elevating the performance of everyone on the team. This philosophy, often referred to as the "Inclusion Rule," highlights the importance of teamwork: Success comes when each person excels in their role to achieve a shared goal. Jackson explained, "You need everybody to feel their role has an opportunity to be displayed."[1]

Any book of mine without a sports analogy is considered incomplete. There are individual sports and team sports. Marrying into a blended family is much like joining a basketball team, where each person's unique skills contribute to a shared goal. Just as a team requires players to understand their roles—whether shooting, defending, or passing—a blended family thrives when each member brings their strengths to the table while working toward unity. Trust and connection, like teamwork, are built over time through consistent effort, clear communication, and mutual support. On the court, victories come not from one player's heroics but from collaboration and adapting to challenges together. Similarly, in a blended family, success is found when everyone feels valued for their individual contributions while striving for a harmonious, loving family dynamic.

A strong blended family is built on a foundation of shared commitment, and that commitment starts with the marriage. As the co-captains of your parenting team, you and your spouse must rely on each other completely to have each other's backs. This means more than just believing in each other's fidelity; it's about trusting each other's judgment in parenting and financial decisions and navigating the other everyday challenges of life. With that solid foundation, you can build the bridge to connect with your stepchildren and foster those individual relationships that create a sense of teamwork within the whole family. But without that initial trust between partners, the foundation is shaky. And just like on the court, where a missed pass or a broken play can disrupt the flow, any cracks in the foundation of trust—whether in your marriage or your relationships with the children—can throw the whole family off balance. Nurturing that dependency is the key to a winning season for your blended family.

Getting Ahead of the Game

Life coach and author Tracee White tells how she and her husband began nurturing trust with each other's children when they became engaged:

> When I met my husband, he told me upfront that he had three children, one of whom has exceptional needs, specifically, Down Syndrome. I wasn't concerned because I always wanted more children.

However, there were parts of this journey that wouldn't be easy, and as we moved forward, I soon realized that this dynamic would require some adjustment for all of us. My husband and I met in March 2021, and we were engaged by July. From that point on, we focused on building organic relationships with each other's children. While I felt confident in my ability to love and support his kids, I did carry an underlying fear of making sure I "got it right" when it came to raising a child with exceptional needs. I wanted to educate myself as thoroughly as possible to ensure I met her unique needs. I took time to learn what I could about Down Syndrome before we were all under one roof.

Besides adjusting to the dynamic of blending our families, we also focused on helping our kids bond as a unit. We spent time together as a family before moving in, doing activities and creating opportunities to be present for the kids in any way possible. We made it clear to the children that our goal was not to replace anyone's parents but to add love and support to their lives. It wasn't always easy, but we approached it with patience and care.

Today, our household includes my husband's twenty-year-old daughter, his eighteen-year-old son, and our two sixteen-year-olds: my son and his daughter with exceptional needs. My oldest son, now twenty-five, lives and works out of state. Although all three of my husband's children share the same mother, only two of them lived with us full-time from the beginning of our marriage. About a year later, we added their youngest child, which meant I was now responsible for the full-time care of a child with exceptional needs.

This experience has been a profound life lesson. It has taught me patience in ways I never imagined, especially since there's so much she can't do for herself, including basic hygiene care. It has also opened my heart in ways I never expected. In addition to bonding with her, I've worked hard to build relationships with my other two bonus children while ensuring my youngest biological son knows he is still incredibly important to me. This balancing act is one of the more difficult, yet often unspoken, challenges of blending families. My youngest son got along well with the other kids but struggled with the idea that his dad and I wouldn't reconcile, all while navigating his own teenage years. Also, because my oldest son had been out of the house for some time, he had grown accustomed to it just being the two of us. This part of the journey hasn't always been easy, but one thing I've learned is to give kids the space to figure things out on their own. Let them know you're there, but don't force anything. Over time, they will come to you.

In addition to building connections within our household, we established joint decision-making early on. This means no child can approach only their biological parent to ask for something without first clearing it with both of us. We implemented this system to prevent them from trying to play us against each other—though, of course, they tried! Eventually, they all learned and followed the rules.

My childhood helped me navigate this journey with grace. I was raised by a father who wasn't my biological parent and gained a deep understanding of the power of unconditional love and acceptance. I witnessed a man love me without hesitation, and even after he and my mom had a biological child together, he never treated me any differently. He and my mother taught me that he was my father, and the way he loved me made that clear. This experience shaped how I approach our blended family today.

Another valuable lesson I learned is the importance of joint decision-making and maintaining a united front between the adults. Along with love and acceptance, we emphasize this unity in our home, which has been crucial for establishing clear boundaries. Over time,

I've built a trusting, loving relationship with the kids, and today, they even call me "Mom."

I'm truly blessed with incredible kids, but that doesn't mean the journey has been without its challenges. Our focus has always been on the children rather than on our own feelings. The key to successfully parenting in a blended household is giving kids the space to work through their emotions while building relationships. They will sometimes feel torn as they try to figure out how to love you without feeling like they're betraying their other parent. Understanding this emotion and being patient with their process has been essential.

Blending families has been a transformative journey full of growth, challenges, and unexpected rewards. While it's not always easy, the effort to meet each child where they are and support them without pushing has allowed us to create a home where everyone feels valued. My experience has taught me that there's no one-size-fits-all approach to parenting, especially in a blended family. It's about showing up consistently, listening, and offering unconditional love while understanding that every child's journey is unique. I've learned that family isn't defined by biology, it's defined by the bonds we nurture and the care we give. And while we may not have all the answers, I am incredibly grateful for the beautiful, blended family we are building together, one day at a time.[2]

The White family is seeing their family win because they laid a foundation of trust and understood that developing meaningful relationships between stepsiblings, stepparents, and biological parents requires time, patience, and effort.

The Scramble Drill

Premarital counseling, advice from seasoned couples, and self-help books are great resources to give you practical ideas about deepening connections in your family. However, even if you have the perfect plays drawn up in your mind, the unique dynamics in a blended family can sometimes feel more like a scramble drill. This is where the learning occurs: in the trenches, in the everyday realities of living life, caring for your home and raising children. In other words, like the last-minute decision made by a basketball player when the play falls apart, you have to follow your gut, learn from your mistakes, and make the right call for the team. Those "game-time decisions" are often about parenting methods, discipline, and dealing with step relationship issues. And just like on the court, trust is crucial. You must believe that your partner has your back and remain confident that you're both working toward the same goal. Together, you can navigate the unexpected plays, weather the rough patches, and come out stronger as a team.

When Calvin and I fell in love and built a life during a global pandemic, it was like constructing a house during a hurricane. Lockdowns, social distancing, and the ever-present fear of illness created an invisible barrier between us and the world, making it incredibly difficult to establish meaningful connections with our soon-to-be bonus children and even our closest friends. Video calls replaced in-person meetings, and the simple joy of gathering with loved ones was a distant memory. We entered our marriage with a foundation of love but delayed the task of building vital relationships with our adult children and our support system, a challenge we navigated amid the chaos and uncertainty of a world turned upside down.

Although the pandemic threw a wrench in most of our relationship-building, we had an easier time connecting with our youngest son. We established a bond while his dad and I were dating, and he still lives with us full-time, so those daily interactions—cheering him on at basketball games and just being present—happened organically. But let's be real, he's a teenager, and teenagers are... well, *weird*. Even without a pandemic, treading those moody waters and building genuine connections can feel like trying to decipher hieroglyphics. Add in the fact that he's eight years younger than his closest sibling, meaning he's been in a bit of a solo orbit for a while, and you've got a recipe for a unique set of challenges. Luckily, those everyday moments—the shared meals, family trips, and the consistent presence—built a bridge to his world. And I learned that if all else fails, get ice cream involved.

There is nothing like giving a little one—and, yes, those unpredictable teenagers—a treat to help ease into a moment to build trust. The car rides to get ice cream can be one of the best ways to connect with your children. On a trip to Dairy Queen, I asked our youngest how he felt about our family and our relationship. I opened up the conversation by telling him I was his age when my mother married my stepfather, how I felt about the change in our family, and that it wasn't easy. To my surprise, he didn't hesitate to share. His cooperation may have had more to do with the anticipation of a Blizzard, but I didn't mind. He confessed there was a time when he hoped his parents would get back together, but he knew now this wasn't going to happen. I reassured him, echoing our previous conversations about how I could never replace his mother. I explained that while my actions might sometimes resemble those of a mother, my role was to come alongside his father to provide love and care in our home. We talked openly about the changes our marriage brought, like new house rules and expectations, acknowledging that adjustment takes time and understanding. I asked him to share his honest feelings about me and our relationship. His response, filled with genuine affection, touched my heart. He expressed his appreciation for my care and support, highlighting the value he placed on our family time. I, in turn, reassured him of my love and encouraged him to come talk to me anytime, even about difficult topics. This raw and authentic exchange forged a deeper connection between us. Today, he's the champion of our family nights and reminds us to prioritize those precious moments in the midst of our busy lives.

His willingness to share his feelings not only brought us closer but also created a blueprint for open communication within our family.

Establishing ties with small children comes more naturally. Babies and toddlers crave affection and readily accept those who provide love and care. While navigating their independence, teenagers still benefit from consistent presence and support within the family home. Even adult children living at home offer regular opportunities for interaction and bonding. However, making friendships with stepchildren who split their time between households is another story altogether. The physical distance and divided attention can create a sense of disconnect, making it harder to establish routines, share experiences, and develop the deep-rooted bonds that form through consistent interaction. Similarly, with adult stepchildren who have already flown the nest, creating meaningful connections requires more intentionality, flexibility, and understanding. The lack of daily contact requires a deliberate, proactive effort to bridge the distance and nurture a sense of belonging within the blended family.

Mixing our adult children didn't happen overnight. Each of them adjusted to our new family dynamic in their own time and way. I hoped the connections we share today would have initially come from proactive efforts on both sides. Instead, they often grew from life's challenges, and not all of them were easy. We formed trusting bonds as

Calvin and I supported our adult children through various situations—offering advice, financial help, a place to return to, or assistance with grandkids. These moments, born out of necessity, became opportunities to forge authentic connections that strengthened our family.

It took a few years to see fruit from the seeds we had sown when we first married. Bringing the family together wasn't a piece of cake. Everyone was new to the team and trying to figure out how we would mesh and get to know one another better. I sensed the awkwardness. We tried not to force interactions, but even in what I thought were unforced settings, the sense of unfamiliarity made everyone feel uneasy. Much of the connection we have now started with intentional decisions to encourage our adult children to come over during larger family functions. Eventually, we established a new tradition of monthly family gatherings to continue to build connections and spend quality time with our adult children who are not in the home with us.

I also asked our adult children to share their thoughts on our blended family—how they felt when they first learned Calvin and I were marrying, how they feel now, and what we could do better as a family.

Our oldest daughter, Kayla, expressed that she really didn't know how to feel about her father's decision to marry. She wished we had involved her and her siblings more, not for their approval but to show that we cared about how they felt. But ultimately, she wanted her father to be happy. Kayla recognizes the genuine love and mutual respect in our relationship. She sees how we've supported each other's children, embracing them as family and creating a more positive experience for everyone. Despite any initial reservations, she believes we all have good intentions and love each other in our own ways. With time, she envisions our family growing even stronger.

Cortez, one of our middle sons, opened up about how he struggled with the adjustment at first. He went on to say, "I was a protective son, and I initially felt uncertain about my mom's marriage to Calvin. However, I trusted her judgment and knew she would only be with someone who treated her well. Now, having formed a bond with Calvin, I'm grateful for everything he has done to make me feel comfortable and the strong relationship we've developed. I like the time our family spends together. Cairo and I are close, and I also want to work on my individual relationships with Kayla and C3."

Our other middle son, Cairo, was away at college during most of our dating and the first year of our marriage. When he returned home briefly, it gave us a chance to have meaningful conversations and deepen our connection. He shared that he was genuinely excited for his dad and appreciated my caring and genuine nature. He feels our marriage has been positive for all of us and hopes we continue spending time together and growing closer as a family.

Like the perspectives of our family members, every blended family's story is unique, with different dynamics, relationships, and journeys from dating to marriage. The day-to-day interactions will vary, and not everyone may embrace the new family dynamic. In fact, some may struggle or never fully come around. However, when biological parents, stepparents, children, and stepsiblings make intentional efforts to form a genuine friendship, it creates opportunities for connection. These efforts lead to a win for everyone, transforming the family into a unified and supportive team.

~BLENDED FAMILIES 101~
Laying the Foundation for Trust and Deeper Connection

What are each of your stepchild's interests, hobbies, and passions?

> Showing genuine interest in a child's world is fundamental to building any relationship, especially with stepchildren. It demonstrates that you value them as individuals and want to connect with them on a personal level. Engage in conversations about their favorite activities, attend their games or performances, and ask questions to show you care. Even small gestures like remembering their favorite food or offering to help with a school assignment can go a long way.

What are your individual love languages, and how can you express love to your stepchild in ways they understand and appreciate?

> Everyone experiences and expresses love differently. Understanding your stepchild's love language (e.g., words of affirmation, acts of service, gifts, quality time, physical touch) allows you to connect with them in ways that resonate and make them feel truly loved. Observe their behavior, ask questions, and learn how they express affection to others. Tailor your actions to their specific language, whether through verbal encouragement, spending quality time together, or offering practical help.

What boundaries and expectations are important for creating a respectful and comfortable relationship between stepparent and stepchild?

Establishing clear boundaries gives a sense of safety and predictability, which is especially important for children. Disagreements are inevitable in any family, but it's good to have healthy conflict-resolution strategies to prevent resentment. Have age-appropriate discussions with expectations around physical touch, privacy, communication, and discipline. It helps prevent misunderstandings and maintain healthy relationships.

How can you create opportunities to bond and build positive memories together?

Shared experiences open the door for lasting connections and provide a sense of family unity. Positive memories lay the foundation for a strong and loving stepparent–stepchild relationship. Plan regular activities that everyone enjoys, whether it's family game nights, movie marathons, or weekend outings. Be present and engaged during these activities. Focus on having genuine connections and creating happy memories.

CHAPTER FOUR

Managing Different Parenting Styles

"Also, unity is not the absence of disagreement but a consensus to agree to work together."
—Dr. Ian Traill

Politics is like pumpkin spice during the fall season—either you love it or are convinced it ruins everything. It evokes strong emotions and opinions that have caused division from the lowest to the highest levels of society. You either avoid political conversations like the plague or dive into them for a healthy debate, which, if you're not careful, can turn into the royal rumble. For me, politics is about as interesting as watching paint dry. I know just enough about politics in the United States not to be dangerous but to make an informed, educated vote. That said, while the media paints a stark picture of the different political parties being at war with one another, no matter what political party holds office, laws are enacted in this country through joint efforts and management of conflicting views of people within the executive branch agencies. At the highest level, the president and vice president, while within the same political party, are two unique individuals who may agree on the high-level beliefs of the party but have perspectives and values that may conflict with one another. Yet, despite their differences in background and beliefs, they find common ground to lead the nation. This level of partnership demonstrates that we can achieve unity and progress despite deep-seated differences.

Like politics, conflicting parenting styles are common, regardless of family type, and can cause great division between parents. Your upbringing and personality play a big part in how you show up as a parent. Blended families must navigate the complexities of intertwining their values, attitudes, expectations, and affection for their children—both biological children and stepchildren.[1] During the engagement phase of the relationship, so much focus is given to the chemistry, compatibility, beliefs, and future plans of the couple that even premarital counseling can fall short of focusing on how the new couple will work together to raise their children. Kids are full of surprises. Unless they express their displeasure about the happy couple's union before the marriage, most parents are ill-prepared for how kids may respond to changes in the family structure and home. And children aren't the only ones who drop bombshells when two families merge and disagreements arise about parental decisions. Parents and stepparents may have different approaches to discipline, rules, and routines that cause confusion and potential conflict within the household.

None of us fit perfectly into personality types and parenting styles, but we inherently fall into patterns that represent what we do most of the time. Understanding the basics can help blended families thrive despite differing parenting preferences. Traditional families may ignore discussions about parenting styles because it's assumed that married biological parents will naturally "figure it out." On the other hand, blended families often have the privilege of discussing expectations. The adults can agree on core values and rules that both parents can support, even if their methods differ. This provides consistency for the children.

Presenting a Cohesive Front

I helped raise my spouse's younger children in both of my blended families. In my first marriage, my son's father and I worked opposite shifts, which minimized co-parenting challenges since I had primary responsibility for our son and his stepbrother. When I remarried, my son was already an adult living on his own, so my husband wasn't involved in his upbringing; but my youngest bonus son, a teenager, is in the home with us. Blending our lives and parenting styles hasn't always been easy, and I've learned a lot along the way.

In my previous co-parenting arrangement, we cohabitated before marriage, an approach I wouldn't recommend. Cohabitation can blur boundaries and give a false sense of commitment, which may complicate the process of building a strong, lasting foundation for marriage. My bonus son had been in my life from a young age, and we formed a close bond before my biological son's birth. My bonus son was six years older than my son and was with us every other weekend, with more extended periods during school breaks. Due to work schedules and my ex-husband's passive parenting style, we rarely overlapped in rule-setting or decision-making, which kept the peace and made the transition after marriage relatively smooth. When I say "smooth," I don't mean it was by design—it was more a matter of circumstance. As the stepparent, I took on most of the discipline, rule-setting, and activities in our daily routine. This wasn't ideal—it created an imbalance that made cohabitation feel more comfortable than intentional and gave us little reason to step back and evaluate how we were doing as both partners and parents when we decided to marry. Even with premarital counseling, we weren't motivated to examine what did and didn't work in our parenting styles. Our different approaches didn't spark tension. Instead, they created silence—a silence that ultimately became a barrier in our relationship.

Fortunately for my bonus son, our relationship with his mother and her husband was unique; we all communicated exceptionally well, and our top priority was always the children's best interests. When we disagreed, we relied on shared values and fairness to achieve a balanced outcome. Most people could hardly believe that we got along so well. Disagreements didn't come in the form of challenging parenting styles. There were minor issues, such as who would have my bonus son for special dates and holidays. His mother and stepfather were solid in handling the day-to-day responsibilities and regularly involved us with school-related and social activities.

Our biggest challenge came when his mother and I gave birth the same year, moving his child position from the youngest to the middle in both homes. It was a big adjustment for him, but we didn't see any abnormal reactions. Competing for attention with a new sibling isn't unusual for any family type. Shared values, similar house rules, and expectations between our two homes made a big difference and contributed to a consistent approach he enjoyed for much of his life. Overall, he was a good kid. Both his mother's husband and I had been in his life since he was three years old, and I was fortunate enough to maintain a relationship with him after their father and I divorced. Age can significantly affect a child's response to changing family dynamics. The younger a child is, the more likely they will accept the stepparent. Children under ten may adjust more easily to blended families because they thrive on cohesive family relationships.[1]

The blended family can be hard to manage when your kids are in their teen years. They might look more grown-up than younger children, but they need love, encouragement, and regular direction just as deeply. In my own experience, my bonus son, C3, was eleven when I married his father. We were fortunate that the pandemic, despite its disruptions, allowed for a gradual transition. Life slowed down, and we naturally fell into a rhythm where my husband took the lead on discipline and daily routines.

But friction slowly reared its head as the initial ease of our blended family life faded. C3's behavior shifted, demanding more active discipline, and suddenly, my husband and I found ourselves navigating uncharted territory. We stumbled through disagreements, frustrated by the seemingly impossible task of finding a unified approach. Should we ground him for a week or simply have a conversation? Was this defiance or typical teenage angst? These questions seemed simple but became obstacles as our individual parenting styles clashed. Looking back, those clashes, though uncomfortable, ultimately strengthened our bond. We were, and still are, committed to talking through every disagreement, no matter how we feel. We made a pact early on: Peace reigns in our home. This meant swallowing our pride, listening to each other, and making an agreement that worked for us both. It is a pact grounded in the fact that our marriage is a covenant, impermeable to the cyclones of family drama.

This pledge to our family makes us humble, which is wonderful. When you're in the throes of a conflict, it's easy to get defensive and see only your own side. But pushing ourselves to hear what the other person has to say and to see how they are influenced by the experience has been transformative. It's not just about finding a solution; it's about empathy and deepening our connection with our son and one another. In our family, encouraging transparency and mutual respect is the norm—even with our now-adult kids. The door's always open, though we can't drag them through it kicking and screaming if they're not ready to talk.

However, not everyone is this fortunate. When parents consistently fail to find common ground in their parenting approaches, the consequences can be significant. Children become confused and insecure, feeling caught in a tug-of-war between conflicting expectations and inconsistent discipline. This can lead to resentment, acting out, and even manipulation as children learn to exploit the discrepancies between parents. Imagine a child going from a home with strict rules and early curfews to one with an inconsistent bedtime and unlimited screen time. Or conversely, imagine a child used to leniency suddenly facing a rigid schedule and harsh consequences for minor infractions. This inconsistency undermines a child's sense of stability and can lead to resentment toward one or both parents and the new family dynamic.

Going back to our politics analogy, a foundational component of our government is working together with opposing views to do what is in the best interest of the country. Similarly, navigating different parenting styles within a blended family can be like walking a tightrope. Fortunately, in our case, while our parenting approach differs significantly from C3's mother, he lived with us full-time, and we aligned on the fundamental parenting decisions for his life. We recognized that our households operated differently, but we respected each other's right to parent as we saw fit as long as our parenting styles caused no harm. This mutual respect, coupled with strong communication between my husband and me, allowed us to present a united front to our son. We made a conscious effort to back up each other's decisions, even if we privately disagreed, and yes, we've missed the mark. If a conflict arose, my husband communicated directly with C3's mother, striving to find common ground while always prioritizing C3's best interests. Of course, sometimes we just went with the flow to keep the peace. And there were some things that went on in our house that his mom did not like and neither did he. But that's how blended families flow when both parents are involved.

It's not an easy route, however. Kids are sensitive; even the smallest parenting variations can lead to confusion and insecurity. Think of a child who receives conflicting messages about screen time, bedtime, or proper punishment for bad behavior. These differences cause worry and frustration as children learn to pit parents against one another. And if parents aren't on the same page, it can strain co-parenting. Differing can turn into arguing, destabilizing trust and cooperation. Not only does this add to the stresses of the adults involved, but it also damages the child's feelings of stability and safety. Parents must have clarity, understanding, a shared dedication to the child's well-being, and ongoing conversations to make it over these hurdles.

In contrast, children are more secure when parents take the same direction. Different styles can help children see many different perspectives. One parent may be a patient and empathetic person, and the other one a disciplinarian and a structured worker. Under the right conditions, this combination gives children empathy and accountability as they learn to gain independence and boundaries. To make this scenario work, parents need to communicate regularly and find common ground to ensure they present a unified front. In the end, aligning values and expectations is key to creating an environment where both kids and parents feel secure and supported.

Discipline: The Struggle Should Be Real

Differing views on discipline can cause major conflict in blended families. Disagreements over spanking, acceptable language, punishments, and other approaches can damage the stepparent–stepchild relationship and the biological parent–biological child relationship and give rise to tension between partners. Couples should discuss and agree on who takes the lead in disciplining each other's children to ensure child safety, avoid resentment, and maintain consistency in the home.

Discipline is a delicate and crucial matter that requires intentionality and respect for relationships. In my experience, physical punishment has never played a role—neither by my stepfather nor by me as a bonus mom. In both of my blended family situations, the biological parents served as the primary disciplinarians, while my role centered on administering consequences when necessary, either collaboratively or independently, in the absence of the biological parent. My biological son never had a stepparent when he was younger, so I didn't face the challenge of navigating disciplinary roles. Stepparents must approach discipline, especially physical forms, with caution. I agree with family therapist and author Ron Deal's insight:

One of the limitations on spanking is who can do it. Newly adoptive parents, foster parents, stepparents who are new on the scene and just beginning to develop a relationship with a child—it's advisable that they not use spanking. It's your bond and trust with a child that gives credibility to the message behind spanking. And if you're still working on the bond, you need to stay away from it.[2]

A couple may even agree that the stepparent shouldn't conduct any form of discipline with their partner's biological child. Instead, to avoid disagreements, they may prefer that the stepparent bring the issue to the biological parent to address. This approach can be a good compromise as long as behaviors and situations are addressed in ways that satisfy both parents.

There is a plethora of research about violence against children. Family structure is one factor the research explores. More specifically, studies have examined the possibility that certain types of families, such as stepfamilies and single-parent families, pose a greater risk of violence to children compared with families headed by both biological parents. Apart from scientific evidence, stepparents are commonly thought of by society as more punitive and abusive than genetic parents. Although some studies have investigated lethal and nonlethal violence perpetrated by stepparents, most research on violence against children has not distinguished between genetic parents and stepparents. In addition, it is difficult to isolate stepparent status as a risk factor for violence against children because stepfamilies face a particularly high volume of problems and challenges, which may serve as contributing factors to violence against children.[3]

I know a blended family led by a couple who has been married for over twenty years. The wife brought three biological children into the marriage, and the two share a child together. The stepfather was allowed to spank and discipline his stepchildren. There was rebellion early on, but later in life, those now-adult children—two sons and a daughter—express appreciation and gratitude for how they were raised. They have an endearing respect for their stepfather. I can't speak to whether or not they felt any resentment for the way they were disciplined, but I know the stepfather did his best to balance the relationship with love, raising each of his stepchildren as if they were his own biological children.

Even if the biological parent and stepparent agree that spanking or other forms of discipline are acceptable, they must know that their spouse has their child's best interest at heart and would never intentionally harm them. Care and connection should always take precedence; they form the foundation for effective discipline and a harmonious family dynamic.

Much like finding common ground in politics, managing different parenting styles requires collaboration, compromise, and a commitment to shared goals. Parents in a blended family must balance their unique perspectives and approaches to effectively raise children together. Parenting styles may clash, but when both partners focus on what's best for the family, they create a foundation for unity and stability. This effort not only strengthens the parental partnership but also shows the children how to work through differences with respect and understanding. By managing conflicting styles thoughtfully, blended families can build a home environment where everyone thrives.

~BLENDED FAMILIES 101~
Finding Common Ground and Having Consistent Rules

How were you disciplined as a child, and how do you think that influenced your current parenting style?

Understanding how your childhood discipline shaped your parenting style is important for building a healthy blended family. Reflecting on your past helps you identify patterns you want to replicate or avoid, uplifting self-awareness and breaking potentially harmful cycles. This introspection promotes empathy and understanding within the family, creating a nurturing environment for all children. Examining your past discipline also helps you recognize potential triggers and biases, allowing you to respond more calmly and constructively in challenging situations.

How can you openly and honestly discuss your different parenting styles without judgment?

Openly discussing your different parenting styles creates a unified front and forms consistent expectations. You can initiate these conversations by focusing on understanding, not criticism; emphasizing the importance of compromise; and finding common ground. It's about listening, feeling, and speaking with respect when it comes to such potentially intimate conversations. If done well, these conversations can create more respect between husbands and wives, minimize conflict, and give the children a greater sense of security. Ultimately, this collaborative approach to parenting builds a stronger, more cohesive blended family.

What are your non-negotiable values, and where are you willing to be flexible when it comes to raising children?

Identifying your non-negotiable values as a couple helps lay a consistent foundation for raising children. Start by listing your own core values, then discuss and prioritize them with your spouse. Look for common ground and areas for flexibility. This process helps establish clear expectations and boundaries, which reduces conflict and confusion for everyone. When you know each other's values, you respect each other, and your relationship becomes stable for the kids. By recognizing areas of flexibility, you can adapt and accommodate different parenting styles and make your blended family work better for you.

What strategies can you use to communicate effectively about parenting disagreements?

Effective communication techniques are critical for healthy and respectful blended family relationships when parenting conflicts arise. Set rules and schedule a neutral time and place to talk about disagreements gently and constructively, out of the children's reach. Agree to find an answer together, respect each other's point of view, and compromise. When your communication is healthy, you can teach your children how to deal with conflict, and you become more effective co-parenting partners. Consider the situations below and how you and your family can better handle disagreements.

- When deciding on bedtime rules, acknowledge each other's perspective and agree on a consistent time that balances flexibility with structure.
- If one parent disciplines differently, discuss the approach privately and present a united front to the children to avoid confusion or favoritism.
- To manage stepsibling conflicts, listen to all sides and work together to set fair rules. Encourage positive relationships by regularly asking the children to share something they appreciate about each other.
- If one parent feels left out of decision-making, schedule regular check-ins to discuss household rules and responsibilities together.
- When differing opinions arise about screen time, agree to try one plan for a set period and reassess together later.

- If one child feels singled out, have a private conversation about how to ensure consistency in consequences across all children.
- When introducing new traditions, involve everyone in brainstorming to create shared family experiences.
- If disagreements arise about curfews for teens, compromise by setting a curfew with room for adjustment based on responsibility.
- When addressing an ex-spouse's influence, focus on what's best for the children and avoid criticizing the other parent in front of the children.
- During family meetings, when appropriate, give each person a chance to speak and vote on key decisions to encourage collaboration and respect.

CHAPTER FIVE

Co-Parenting and Coping with Ex-Partners

"Co-parenting is not a competition. It is a collaboration of two homes working together with the best interest of the child at heart. Work for your kids, not against them."
—Dr. Anne Brown

You know the story of Cinderella, the girl forced to live as a servant by her cruel stepmother and stepsisters. The good versus evil tale is the old one, and the stepmother is all bad—cold, stingy, and bent on ruining Cinderella's life. This persona—encoded in our popular imagination by fairy tales and their thousand variants—remains a heavy cloud over the world of stepparents, especially stepmothers. It reinforces the stereotype that stepparents are hateful, cruel, and selfish.

But what if it was not quite this simple? What if Cinderella's stepmother wasn't quite so guilty? Perhaps she was bitter because she and Cinderella's father had a strained co-parenting relationship; communication and respect were missing, creating unhappiness that poisoned the family unit. This—and it's something that is often missed in mainstream stories—is what makes co-parenting important. If biological parents can cooperate positively and put their differences aside for the benefit of their children, this is fertile ground on which to grow good stepparent relationships. This chapter focuses on the realities of blended families, how to dispel stereotypes, and how healthy co-parenting can promote having a happy, healthy family life for all.

Let's redefine co-parenting. While many associate co-parenting with pleasant collaboration, the prefix "co" simply means "together with." It implies shared responsibility, not necessarily agreement or camaraderie. Think of it like having a coworker on a project. You might not like them, agree with their methods, or even enjoy their presence. But you still have a shared goal that requires cooperation. Co-parenting is similar. A shared responsibility binds you and your ex-partner: your child's well-being. This doesn't require friendship or liking each other. It demands a mature commitment to putting your child's needs first, even if you clash with your co-parent on a personal level.

In general, co-parenting refers to divorced or separated parents who continue to raise their children together even after they have parted ways. Co-parenting also exists in blended families—one parent is biological and the other is a stepparent, and both actively raise their children together.

According to Michael Vallejo, a licensed clinical social worker, there are three major types of co-parenting: cooperative, conflicted, and parallel.[1]

Cooperative Co-Parenting: In this arrangement, both parents work together to make decisions about raising their children. They communicate regularly, ensuring the children spend quality time with both parents, and they share information about the children's needs. Cooperative co-parenting also involves mindful parenting. In this case, co-parents do their best to interact respectfully so they can make decisions about where the children will live, visitation schedules, and arrangements for their children's education, healthcare, religion, after-school activities, and social activities.

Conflicted Co-Parenting: In this arrangement, parents struggle with poor communication and frequent conflicts. They often differ in parenting styles, schedules, rules, and priorities, and may not agree on their child's upbringing, needs, or daily routine. While raising their children together, their inability to get along can negatively affect the kids, who may feel caught in the middle of their parents' disputes.

Parallel Co-Parenting: In this arrangement, parents function independently, minimizing communication and interaction with each other. Each parent may have their own rules and routines at home, which can create some inconsistencies for the children. This approach is best suited for situations where parents are unable to repair their relationship and often involve their children in conflicts. When frequent arguments or tension occur, parallel parenting can be a healthier option for everyone involved.

In my book, *S.P.I.L.L.—Single Parents Inspiring Love & Legacy*, I wrote about co-parenting because it is near and dear to my heart:

> Even if you have never been married or if you are divorced, co-parenting well, which I will now label as "cooperative co-parenting," is one of the best gifts you can give your children if you are not going to be together as a couple. It is an entirely selfless act for two parents to work together respectfully to do what is in the best interest of your children. Co-parenting may not always be possible depending on the circumstance, but if you can create a successful cooperative co-parenting relationship, there are significant benefits for your children.[2]

It was just me and my son against the world for thirteen years. His father left when he was six, leaving a void that I filled with fierce determination. I was a single mother, navigating the challenges of parenthood solo, never having to experience the complexities of another woman raising my child or the delicate dance of co-parenting with an ex-partner. I was always driven and motivated by a single, powerful ingredient—my love for my son. It was pure, unadulterated, and entirely my responsibility to provide. The few times my son's father made an appearance in his life, the outcome was never a commitment to intentionally stay engaged or be fully present. The door was always open for him to have a relationship with our son. His death, when my son was just sixteen, extinguished any chance of reconciliation between them or any opportunity for a co-parenting experience.

I grew up with limited exposure to healthy co-parenting. My own blended family experiences involved stepfathers who struggled to collaborate with their ex-partners. Despite this, I instinctively cared for my bonus children with the same compassion I'd want for my own son. This doesn't necessarily mean instant love, though that can be a goal. At the very least, it requires genuine care and concern. Stronger bonds can grow from that foundation. I've maintained respectful relationships with my minor bonus-children's mothers, recognizing that co-parenting success hinges on everyone's ability to prioritize the child's needs above personal feelings. However amicable the relationship, co-parenting requires vigilance and courage, especially when safeguarding your children's well-being. I've seen conflicts stemming from rocky relationships between biological parents before the new family formed. In other cases, tensions arose due to concerns that the stepparent was not treating the child fairly. The thought of someone mistreating your children should be alarming. If that scenario exists, you should address it head-on and handle it appropriately with the biological parent and through the legal system if necessary.

Marrying Calvin introduced a different parenting dynamic for me. While my bonus son spent time with his mother every other weekend and on certain holidays, we had him full-time. Stepping into a full-time stepmother role was a profound shift. Being deeply involved in my bonus son's daily life brought new experiences for all of us.

Beyond the logistics of living together, it reinforced a fundamental belief: All children deserve adults in their lives who genuinely care for them. My love for my stepson wasn't solely a byproduct of loving his father; it stemmed from a deep-rooted conviction that every child deserves to feel safe, valued, and supported.

But these feelings don't negate the challenges of co-parenting. It's like taking care of a shared garden—each parent tends to the same precious plant but with different approaches and experiences. Successful co-parenting requires attentive listening, respectful communication, and a willingness to see the world through the other parent's eyes. For me, this meant treating my stepson with the same care and consideration I'd want for my own biological son. It's an ongoing journey that demands patience, understanding, and a shared commitment to nurturing a thriving environment where all children can flourish.

Adjusting to co-parenting in a blended family was harder than Calvin anticipated:

> For years, I was the sole decision-maker for my children, as they lived with me full-time. They visited their mothers on weekends and during summers, but the day-to-day choices were all mine. Suddenly, I had to consider someone else's input, a partner who brought her own parenting style into the mix. It wasn't easy to reconcile our different perspectives, but I realized that creating harmony required a willingness to compromise. Through trial and error, we learned how to parent with love and balance in a household that respected everyone's needs.

Building love and embracing the new direction for our family required a multi-layered approach to co-parenting. Not only did Calvin and I have to assess our own parenting styles and expectations within our home, but we also had to forge a cooperative co-parenting relationship with his ex-wife. This required open communication, mutual respect, and a shared commitment to placing our son's needs at the forefront. It was a constant process of adjustment, demanding patience, flexibility, and a willingness to see beyond individual perspectives to create a unified front for our son.

Keep Kids at the Center, Not in the Middle

It's natural for parents to feel uneasy about another adult stepping into a significant role in their child's life, even in the most well-meaning blended families. While I don't have personal experience with a stepparent raising my son, I've gathered insights from those who have navigated the trenches of blended family life, offering real-world perspectives on the challenges and triumphs of shared parenting. Their experiences paint a vivid picture of the nuances and adjustments that arise when ex-partners and new families collide, providing valuable lessons for anyone seeking to create a thriving blended family.

Tracee, whose journey I discussed earlier, recounts how she felt about divorcing and co-parenting:

> I became a single mother at twenty. But I wasn't alone for long. By the time my son turned one, I met my first husband, who quickly embraced the role of a father. Having grown up with a stepdad whom I have considered my dad since the age of eight, I deeply appreciated how he loved my son as if he were his own despite having no biological children of his own yet.
>
> I was married to my first husband for thirteen years, and during that time, I gave birth to my second son. Though I never imagined that our marriage would end in divorce, it became clear after thirteen years that we needed to part ways and begin a new chapter as co-parents. Our co-parenting journey didn't start easy, but we both prioritized the well-being of our children above all else. Once we focused less on the difficulties of our past, we found it easier to focus on what was best for our boys. I believe this is important for every divorced parent to

embrace; it's not about the two of you or the failed union but about how to make the transition as seamless as possible for the children that are involved.

A few years after our divorce, my ex-husband remarried, and my children gained a stepmother. I never imagined how I would feel about this, but my primary concern was, and is, how she treated my kids and how they got along. Thankfully, both boys felt comfortable and safe with her, so I never felt concerned. The priority remained on the boys and mirroring healthy relationships for them.[3]

Tracee's desire for her boys to feel comfortable and safe with their stepmother highlights a crucial element of healthy co-parenting: trust. Both parents must believe that the other genuinely cares for their children and would never intentionally cause them harm. This foundation of trust promotes cooperation and a shared focus on the children's well-being. Choosing a partner who truly accepts your children is paramount. Acceptance goes beyond mere tolerance; it's an active embrace of those children as an integral part of the family. While some may merely survive on tolerance, thriving families are built on a foundation of genuine acceptance and love. Without it, resentment festers, and the family dynamic can become a ticking time bomb, waiting to explode once the children reach adulthood. Children deserve a loving and supportive home, free from the torment of a "wicked stepmother" or a "lunatic stepfather." Likewise, stepparents shouldn't be subjected to disrespectful or unruly behavior. It's the biological parent's responsibility to ensure they're not bringing their children into a toxic situation. Ignoring red flags during the dating phase can lead to a tumultuous family life, with the marriage strained and the home transformed into a battleground. Choosing a partner who genuinely cares for and respects your children is crucial for creating a harmonious blended family.

Tracee and her husband, Etoya, are founders of Aligned Faith Coaching. As a licensed counselor, Etoya shares insights from his own co-parenting and blended family experiences:

> My journey to peaceful blended parenting has come with its share of bumps in the road, but it definitely appears that the third time really is a charm. I've been married three times, and each marriage has been blended. My first marriage was to the mother of my three biological children, two girls and a boy. She had a child very young, at age fourteen, so I inherited a teenager who eventually became a teen parent. So, at age twenty-eight, I became a "Paw Paw" before I had my own biological children. I vowed not to have children unless I was married, so I went into the situation with no parenting experience. My wife didn't have a good relationship with her child's father, so I had to navigate that space on my own. While I didn't have experience, I wanted to be the best person I could be while being intentional about trying to connect to her child's father. Her daughter didn't live with us, but she and I were able to form a decent relationship. My wife was a child when she had her child, so she was never really a full-

time parent. That impacted our ability to establish norms for how we would raise the three children we eventually had together. Another major barrier was my wife's enmeshment with her family. As we began raising our kids together, it became difficult to adjust to the level of outside influence. Our marriage lasted nine years but ended in a bitter divorce. Post-divorce, co-parenting didn't change much, but our communication relationship was severely strained. I was an extremely active father and saw my kids every single day, which I continued by any means necessary. The energy didn't shift until I found myself in another relationship, which exacerbated the negative energy and communication with my new ex-wife.

The new relationship grew, and I eventually moved out of state and got remarried. Both of those decisions proved costly. My second wife had a very young son and two teen daughters. My son was six or seven at the time, and he resented me taking on the responsibility for another son. Unfortunately, that difficulty was exacerbated by the negative energy he received from my wife, coupled with my eventual move out of state. My second wife adjusted very well to my two daughters, but, for whatever reason, she couldn't understand what my son was experiencing, and I didn't have the skill or awareness to call it out so we could address the problems. Moving out of state was the worst thing I could ever have done, and it created lasting emotional hurt for my son, which, fortunately, we have overcome and grown from. My second wife had three children by three different men, and each situation had very unique characteristics. Again, I found myself juggling multiple levels of relationship dynamics in a relationship that became codependent. While out of state, I dealt with depression because I'd never been away from my kids. My wife and her children didn't understand what I was dealing with, and there were other stressors affecting the family dynamics. Financial strain from gaps in employment caused resentment with my ex-wife, which she expressed toward my wife as well. Those interactions created conflict between my wife and ex-wife, which trickled down to our co-parenting dynamics, damaging what had become a functional system.

I eventually moved on from the second marriage and discovered a place of peace and balance as a single person, working as a co-parent. My children's mother and I resolved important legal matters, which helped us reduce conflict to some degree. I met my current wife in 2021, and I quickly learned what happens when people take the time to build healthy relationships and find points of agreement. I already had full-time custody of my two older children, both high schoolers, and my youngest daughter visited during the week and every other weekend. While my wife and I were dating, I told her about the rocky relationship with my children's mother. Tracee understood, and we focused solely on building the healthiest relationships we could. My wife has done an exceptional job of helping me manage my own emotions and the challenges of co-parenting. We communicate openly about the relationship dynamics and, thankfully, my kids have an amazing relationship with my wife. She is their mother, and they are her children. My oldest two call her "Mom," which is a testament to her loving approach toward them. She is at every possible game and supports every possible endeavor. And her sons are my sons, and I treat them as such. Their relationship with me is not defined by a title but by my genuine support of them. Our relationship is authentic. Her youngest son is very close with his dad, and I respect their relationship. I respect his dad's role in his life, which comes out in my communication with him. His dad and I can sit at baseball games and wrestling meets and chat like we know each other. Focusing on healthy relationships creates an atmosphere of emotional safety for everyone in the family. Successful family blending happens when people take time to first value the importance of healthy relationships and then attend to each individual relationship. Families who try to grow *all* the relationships often miss the individual needs that are present. Families that work to grow *each* relationship are tuned in to individual needs. If all members of a family are treated equally, none of them are being treated fairly. We were honest with each other about what we were getting into, and we've been successful at communicating and reaching the healthy space we're in today. We understand where boundaries are necessary. We spend time in each other's spaces. We respect differences. We acknowledge successes and grow from opportunities. Blending takes skill, and I'm grateful to be part of a unit that is built so much on love and the genuineness of relationships that it is protected from conflict. It's important for people to be transparent about their co-parenting history so a potential partner can gauge their bandwidth to handle those situations.[4]

As you navigate the uncharted waters of blended family life, remember that you are not alone. Like Etoya and Tracee, countless others have embarked on this journey, facing similar hurdles and celebrating similar triumphs. Embrace your family's uniqueness, celebrate each member's diverse perspectives and experiences, and cherish the opportunity to create something healthy for your family. The path to an effective blended family takes time, patience, and an openness to the unknown. You must communicate honestly, have empathy, and put the kids' needs first. It's about forgetting, forgiving, and choosing to create a future in which we are loved, respected, and able to see the other side.

This stepparent–biological parent interaction is what makes blended families so stable and supportive for children. Respect is paramount and creates the foundation for productive communication and cooperation, all to the children's benefit. The biological parent should not tolerate any abuse of the stepparent from the kids or ex-partner. Such practices undermine the stepparent's authority and presence in the household and can lead to unnecessary tension. Openly addressing issues of disrespect with your ex and children in a constructive manner establishes boundaries that sustain unity and preserve the family's sense of harmony.

At the same time, stepparents need to be cautious, as well, to not say bad things or act in an offensive manner toward the children or former partner. This can break trust, evoke long-term resentment, and undermine the very basis of the blended family. Both parents are responsible for discouraging this behavior and setting an example of respect and maturity. By modeling respect and setting clear boundaries, both the stepparent and biological parent can create a healthier dynamic, fostering an environment where everyone feels valued and supported.

And never forget the wise words that have guided us throughout this book: "Co-parenting is not a competition. It is a collaboration of two homes working together with the child's best interest at heart. Work for your kids, not against them." By keeping this principle at the core of your journey, you'll create a legacy of love, resilience, and ongoing support.

~BLENDED FAMILIES 101~
What Can You Do to Improve Your Co-Parenting Relationships?

What boundaries must be established or enforced with the other biological parent to ensure healthy communication and minimize conflict?

The most important way to set expectations and avoid miscommunication is to have explicit boundaries when dealing with co-parenting conflicts. Discuss communication channels (e.g., email, text, telephone calls), the right topics to discuss, and how to handle conflicts. Seek out a therapist or mediator to set boundaries, especially in a high-conflict scenario.

How can you effectively manage logistical challenges like scheduling, transportation, and sharing information about the children?

Easy operations save everyone time and keep everyone shielded from unnecessary conflict. Maintain shared calendars, a parenting schedule, and specific procedures for tracking health, education, and routines with the children. If you find yourself in a conflicted circumstance, use an external app or website to communicate, keep records, and cut down on face-to-face contact.

Despite different parenting styles, how can you ensure consistent approaches and expectations for the children across both households?

Consistency gives children a sense of stability and predictability, reducing anxiety and confusion. Talk with the other parent about rules, consequences, and expectations, even in parallel co-parenting. Focus on finding common ground and prioritizing the child's needs.

How can you best support each other in your co-parenting roles within your home, especially when dealing with challenging behaviors or situations?

Parenting can be stressful, especially in blended families. A strong support system within your home is important for navigating challenges and maintaining a united front. Create a safe space for discussing parenting struggles and strategies. Offer encouragement, empathy, and practical assistance to each other. Consider seeking professional guidance or counseling if needed.

CHAPTER SIX

Adulting: They May Be Grown, But They're Not Gone

"The job of parenting doesn't end when children reach adulthood; the relationship simply changes."
—*Unknown*

Sitting across from a dear friend over coffee, I couldn't help but smile as she shared her exciting news: She was getting married. Her joy was infectious as she gushed about this amazing gentleman and their upcoming wedding plans. She was still in awe to have found love again in her seventies. We giggled like schoolgirls, discussing the next few months, until our conversation naturally shifted to our children—a familiar topic during our breakfast get-togethers, where we'd catch up on life's highs and lows. Because she was someone I looked up to as a motherly mentor, I always valued her wisdom and insight.

This time, however, her tone grew somber. She confided that while her son, who lived locally, was thrilled about her marriage, her adult daughter, living out of state, was far from pleased. My friend was heartbroken and blindsided by her reaction, especially since the friction disrupted plans for my friend to move closer to her daughter. What she had expected to be a joyful season instead brought a period of tension and unexpected challenges in their relationship. Though her daughter eventually came around to accept her decision, the journey was a painful reminder of how adult children can struggle with change, even when it involves their parent's happiness.

It's often surprising to realize how much adjustment adult children may need when their parent decides to remarry, no matter their age or stage in life. This is why it's so important to acknowledge the unique challenges blended families face, particularly the impact on adult children. I've witnessed firsthand the heartbreaking strain this can cause—sometimes leading to major breaches in relationships, where adult children sever ties or stop speaking to their parent altogether. While every parent hopes such rifts are temporary, the reality is that these situations can create deep separation that isn't easily repaired.

There are times when adult children may have valid concerns, and in healthy parent–child relationships, these should be expressed with love, respect, and openness to the parent's decision. Unfortunately, not all responses come from a place of maturity, and disapproval can manifest in ways that feel like an adult tantrum, causing pain and broken connections. Navigating this delicate dynamic requires patience, understanding, and intentional effort to rebuild trust and communication, hoping to find common ground and restore the bond.

Most people are very surprised to learn that adult stepfamilies (those formed in the second half of life that include adult stepchildren) have just as many transitions as stepfamilies with younger children. Some of the transitional issues are different, but many are the same.[1] If possible, it is important to encourage consistent interactions with adult stepchildren, even when they no longer live at home. These bonds become invaluable during life's challenges, offering support and understanding rooted in shared experiences and the unique dynamics of a blended family. By nurturing these relationships, we create an extended family network—a source of belonging and stability that reaches far beyond the walls of the household. This realization gave me the heart to see other blended families embrace intentionality and thrive in their journeys, ensuring every member feels valued and connected.

Not Just Theory, I Really Do Understand

My mother got married again when I was in my early twenties. I was still at home then, and I tagged along when they bought a house together. My second stepfather was a cool and laid-back guy. We never had any conflicts, but we also didn't form a deep bond. He had a much younger son from a previous relationship, but I never connected with him either.

Living under my mother and stepfather's roof as an adult required adjustment, but I respected their home and rules. Focused on work and school, I had little time for anything else. When my mother asked me to contribute financially, it was a fair request. However, it also sparked a desire for complete independence. If I could afford to pay her, then I could afford to be on my own, too. That became my catalyst, propelling me toward self-sufficiency and the next chapter of my life.

My time living in their home was short-lived. Shortly after my mother and stepfather married, I moved in with my best friend from high school. Looking back, I didn't have a strong positive or negative response to my mother's remarriage. He seemed to make her happy, and I was content as long as she was happy. My mother had always taught me to be independent, so I didn't rely on her for financial support or much problem-solving once I moved out. I would see my stepfather when I visited my mother, and our interactions were always cordial, but we never developed a close relationship. A few years later, my mother and stepfather separated and eventually divorced. I didn't harbor any negative emotions about their separation. Instead, I felt a sense of indifference. Their relationship had run its course, and I accepted their decision.

Navigating my mother's second marriage as a young adult profoundly shaped my understanding of blended families. At the time, I felt indifferent, perhaps as a defense mechanism against the heartbreak I'd seen in relationships that didn't last. Over the years, however, my perspective evolved as I observed blended families with meaningful connections with their adult children and experienced the beginnings of such bonds with my younger bonus children. These early efforts laid the foundation for how I desire to interact and connect with my children as they grow into adulthood and taught me the importance of intentionality in building those relationships.

In chapter three, I shared the heartfelt and sometimes complicated reactions from Calvin's and my adult children to our decision to marry. We had many conversations about our children before blending our lives, but looking back, it's clear that we couldn't fully anticipate the challenges we'd face in navigating our childrens' adult lives as a newly blended family. The truth is, while our middle sons were technically adults—with one in college and the other still searching for his path in life—they were adults in age only. What we discovered, often through difficult circumstances, was that they needed far more parental engagement and oversight than we had realized.

These revelations didn't come all at once but through troubling events that unfolded as we settled into our new life together. From missed opportunities to make responsible choices to moments when their emotional struggles came to light, it became clear that they still needed guidance, structure, and sometimes tough love. Calvin and I had to recalibrate our approach, learning to parent collaboratively while respecting each other's roles. Stepping into a fatherly or motherly role requires patience, understanding, and the willingness to navigate moments of resistance or uncertainty. These experiences taught us that "adult" doesn't always mean ready or independent—it's a journey, not a destination. As we worked through these challenges, we found that the investment in their growth, not their pockets, strengthened our relationship with them and our bond as a couple and as a family. Parenting, whether in a blended family or not, can be tough when figuring out when to help your adult children or let them face the consequences of their choices. These times can be filled with moments of second-guessing and the deep desire to shield them from pain or failure. Yet, as hard as it is, we know that stepping in too much can enable them and rob them of the growth that comes from learning through their own experiences. The truth is that love sometimes means standing back, even when every fiber of your being wants to intervene. It's not easy, but allowing them to navigate life's challenges equips them with resilience, accountability, and the confidence to handle what comes their way.

Whether it's adult children returning home, needing significant financial help, or seeking emotional or medical support, parenthood doesn't stop when kids turn twenty-one. In a blended family, these situations can introduce unique challenges, and your spouse may feel the weight of what some might perceive as an added burden. This often means accepting emotional and logistical challenges and the "baggage" that comes with stepping into a supportive role for someone else's adult children.

Navigating these dynamics is rarely burden-free. Pre-existing relationships between the biological parent and their adult children can add layers of complexity, especially if there's tension or estrangement. For a stepparent, stepping into this role can feel particularly daunting, and even in families with established respect and strong ties, building a deep, authentic bond takes patience, understanding, and time. The journey requires compassion, good communication, and the openness to navigate obstacles together to create a sense of unity and shared purpose within the family.

I understand that some biological parents take an authoritative stance, believing they don't need to hear their adult children's opinions or seek their approval when deciding to marry or remarry and creating a blended family. While that perspective is valid, I encourage you to consider another approach—one rooted in mutual respect. Inviting your adult children into the conversation, even if only to share your plans and hear their thoughts, can go a long way in easing potential tensions. This doesn't mean asking for permission but rather demonstrating that their feelings matter and that you value their place in your life. This step can soften the blow of such a significant transition and lay the groundwork for a peaceful family dynamic.

Family Life, an organization dedicated to helping families focus on what matters most, shares valuable guidelines for older parents and stepparents. They emphasize that adult stepchildren, regardless of their age, often experience a range of emotions and thoughts during the blending of a family.[1]

- Children may fear abandonment or losing their connection to their only remaining parent. Having already experienced deep grief, your remarriage could potentially rekindle or amplify those feelings of sadness.[1]

- Adult children often feel a deep loyalty to their original family; maintaining that sense of identity is important to them. Accepting a stepparent can be challenging because it requires adjusting long-standing family dynamics and traditions, including holidays and celebrations, to accommodate someone new. This process can be painful and unsettling. It's important not to take it personally—it's less about you and more about the sense of "home" feeling unfamiliar and changed.[1]

- Children may feel a sense of disloyalty toward their divorced or deceased parent and struggle with guilt over allowing a stepparent to become part of their lives.[1]
- Children may feel jealous or replaced by their parent's new partner. Once the center of their parent's attention, they might now see the stepparent as the one who occupies their parent's heart, time, and energy.[1]
- Worries about family finances are common and need to be addressed thoughtfully. Adult stepchildren often have legitimate concerns about how their family inheritance will be handled, and this isn't about greed—it's about understanding and reassurance. Being proactive in discussing these financial matters can help ease their concerns and provide clarity, fostering trust and peace of mind for everyone involved.[1]
- When one parent of an adult child has passed away, it's common for the surviving parent to focus on ensuring their children have a strong relationship with the remaining grandparent. However, a new marriage can disrupt this dynamic, leading to feelings of resentment. The adult child may feel that their children aren't receiving the time and attention they had hoped for from their parent, creating a sense of loss for everyone involved.[1]

As a new couple, you must apply patience and understanding to these strong emotions. Do not be offended by them. When confronted with difficult responses from adult children, assume a humble position and listen to their fears and concerns. Accept them where they are and try to be responsive to their need for information, emotional contact, and time as they adjust to yet another family transition they didn't seek out.[1]

~BLENDED FAMILIES 101~
Blending Adult Children into the Family

What are your individual expectations for your relationship with your adult children after you blend your family?

Discussing the level of involvement, how often you have contact, and the level of emotional support each partner currently has with their own children helps identify the type of relationship that exists. You may want to create boundaries and discuss responsibilities and the level of authority each partner feels comfortable exercising with their stepchildren. Sharing insights beyond what the future spouse can see for themselves can help them understand you and gives both of you the opportunity to have open and honest communication. It helps define roles and avoid misunderstandings or overstepping.

What are your views on financial support for your adult children, and how might that change within a blended family context?

Being on the same page financially can be a struggle on its own, and providing financial support for your adult children can be a major issue. It's best to address money matters prior to marriage, but even if you must press pause during the marriage, it is important to address potentially sensitive issues like ongoing financial assistance, inheritance plans, and the division of resources. It encourages transparency and proactive planning and can prevent future conflicts.

How can you create a welcoming and inclusive environment for both sets of adult children within your blended family?

You want to create a sense of belonging and acceptance for all members of the new family unit. Include adult children in discussions about shared traditions, family gatherings, and ways to create opportunities for bonding. If adult children are excluded or not given due attention, this can lead to bitterness and conflict. Providing a welcoming space in which everyone can be heard and seen is less likely to trigger these negative feelings and instead promotes steps toward a healthy response.

How can you support your adult children while also respecting their independence and autonomy?

Even when facing challenges, adult children need to feel empowered to make their own choices and navigate their lives independently. Offer guidance and support without being overly controlling or intrusive. Respect their decisions, even if you disagree. Avoid lecturing and provide a safe space for them to seek advice or share concerns with you and their stepparent.

CHAPTER SEVEN

The Marriage Must Stand

"Children are a temporary assignment."
—Jimmy Evans

Imagine a sandwich. The "meat" is the precious journey of raising children in a blended family. But it's the two slices of bread—the biological parent and stepparent—that hold everything together. Without both, the sandwich falls apart. Your marriage, that bond between the slices, must remain strong, enduring sleepless nights with infants, teenage angst, and the bittersweet launch of young adults into the world. It's important to remember that raising children is a temporary assignment—a season that, while deeply meaningful, will eventually end. Those years of raising toddlers and teenagers are fleeting, with unpredictable circumstances and memories; they won't last forever. Soon, the children will come of age, go away, and have their own lives.

Do you remember the list from chapter 1 of the top reasons second marriages might fail at a high rate? The top three were money, sex, and in-laws, and they are the top for why even first-time marriages may fail. Juggling finances; intimacy after long, busy days; and maintaining healthy boundaries with ex-partners are some of the topics that need to be at the top of our agenda for mixing well in our blended marriage and families.

Divorce leaves a mark not only on the couple but on the children and extended family who are left in the dust. When a couple goes into remarriage, there's even more at stake. And, if this new relationship goes wrong, the pain of instability and fracture will continue as children suffer even more loss and separation. Another divorce can also cause feelings of insecurity and relationship mistrust among those children. That's why a blended family's marriage must be more than just surviving—it must be thriving. It's the glue that keeps everything from falling apart again.

A strong, committed marriage breaks this cycle by modeling what healthy relationships look like. It teaches kids that love is permanent, that obstacles can be conquered, and that commitment isn't always perfection but requires hard work. Kids see their parents respect one another as they talk, fight, and make choices—and that's a whole new page in the history of what a family and marriage can be. For couples who've experienced the heartbreak of divorce, this new marriage becomes a chance to rebuild not just their own lives but to reshape the legacy they're leaving for their children.

Making your marriage a priority isn't just about you as a couple—it's about the future. Your children, both your biological children and stepchildren, are watching closely. They need to see that relationships, while challenging, are worth investing in. They need to feel the security of knowing that the foundation of their blended family is strong and unwavering. When the marriage holds, it offers them refuge, a constant in the midst of all the transitions and adjustments they've faced. It tells them that no matter how the story begins, it doesn't have to end in more brokenness.

It's important to know that making your marriage a priority isn't selfish. It's necessary. Parents who have divorced or come out of a cohabitation relationship must understand that their new or current marriage, whatever stage it's in, must take precedence over every external distraction or conflict. Yes, there will be bills, busy schedules, ex-spouses, and parenting challenges. But if the marriage isn't nurtured, everything else begins to crumble. By making your relationship the cornerstone, you create a safe space for everyone—a place where love, trust, and stability aren't just temporary but are built to last. It's a gift not only to yourselves but to your children and the generations that will follow.

Make Your Marriage Work

My first chapter, "Before the Two Become One," is about how we must marry in a healthy state of mind and heart. As we try to be whole, there is no such thing as perfect. We are all humans with our own individual blend of memories, flaws, and scars. No amount of self-work is without unforeseen difficulties in any family. Anger can erupt, doubts may rumble, and unexpected issues such as an affair or secrets can shatter the rock under your feet. This is where the power of your individual "emotional preparedness" really does kick in.

When you've had time to work through wounds, see where you are vulnerable, and develop emotional fortitude, you'll be more prepared for the storms. You'll be able to talk about it, confront problems in a kind way, and reach out for help as needed. You won't slip back into your old patterns or project hurts from the past onto your partner. Consider it like the construction of a house. A good base to support you against turbulence is a must. Your emotional well-being is that bedrock. It gives your relationship a chance to weather whatever might come your way and gives your blended family a safe and secure home to settle into.

Although entering marriage with emotional wholeness won't make it painless, it will give you the fortitude and understanding to get through the bumps along the way. It helps you approach adversity with grace, knowledge, and a desire to evolve as a person and as a couple.

That perspective has a ripple effect and makes your blended family healthier and more durable.

While waiting on our table for dinner one night, Calvin nudged me and said, "Look." Across from us was an elderly couple sitting close together, holding hands. I thought it was the cutest thing ever. I also thought that it was very sweet that it captured my husband's attention. We both just sat there smiling because that is what we consider a marriage goal. As much as we want to accomplish in this life, God willing, we want to grow old together, still loving and liking each other and holding hands. Marrying later in life, we realize that life is short, and we want to make the most of the time we have together after our youngest son leaves our home.

There are "marriage musts" that Calvin and I have committed to, no matter what is happening around us or within our home. These are intentional habits we've agreed to hold each other accountable to because they help us remain close, foster peace in our family, and ensure that our hearts heal after disagreements. Whether it's making time to check in even when things seem to be going well, praying together and engaging in marriage devotionals, seeking professional help when needed, or prioritizing date nights, all of these habits make our relationship healthy and enjoyable. To us, these "musts" are anchors that remind us that we're there for one another and for the family we have been working so hard to create.

Calvin and I have our own list of "marriage musts," but we know that every couple is unique and must discover what works best for their relationship. What strengthens one marriage might not work for another, but the key is finding shared values and intentional habits that bring you closer, especially during the hard times. Every marriage has struggles, but small acts of kindness can make all the difference when a couple prioritizes unity. It could be as simple as leaving a thoughtful note, making time for a heartfelt conversation, or offering a hug after a disagreement. These shared efforts create a foundation of trust, helping you weather the storms together. Ultimately, it's about building a marriage that feels safe—a partnership rooted in love and compassion, ready to take on anything life throws your way.

A blended family marriage requires a level of intentionality that goes beyond what many might expect. Without conscious effort, unresolved wounds or past patterns can quietly creep back in and threaten to repeat the cycle of brokenness. A spouse may still be grieving the death of their previous partner, and those feelings of loss can resurface in unexpected ways. This grief may manifest as emotional distance, difficulty fully investing in the new marriage, or challenges in forming bonds with stepchildren. The unresolved grief can also create tension, as the surviving spouse may unintentionally compare their new relationship to the past one, affecting their ability to fully embrace their blended family.

Calvin and I know that building a successful marriage in a blended family isn't just about avoiding another divorce—it's about breaking generational patterns, showing our children what commitment and love look like, and creating a foundation they can rely on. We often remind ourselves that our marriage isn't just for us—it's for everyone in our family who depends on the stability we create together. This level of commitment doesn't happen by chance; it requires work, patience, and a shared vision. In our home, we've learned that love is less about grand gestures and more about the small, intentional acts that say, "I'm here, and I'm not going anywhere." It's about carving out moments in the chaos to reconnect, choosing to listen instead of arguing, and remembering that we're on the same team even when life feels overwhelming. A strong marriage gives our family its anchor, ensuring that no matter how complicated or challenging things get, we have each other to lean on. When we choose to prioritize our marriage, we're choosing to invest in the future—not just for ourselves but for our children and the legacy of love and resilience we hope to leave behind.

While I might be a whiz with a Ninja blender, I'll confess, my skills as a mixologist are still a work in progress—let's just say some of my creations are more "experimental" than a perfect blend of flavors every time! Sometimes the flavors clash, sometimes they complement, and sometimes they come together to create something entirely unexpected and delightful. Like a smoothie, each person in your blended family brings their own unique ingredient to the mix, some bold and tangy, others smooth and mild. But unlike my carefully measured smoothie recipes, where I can control every ingredient and tweak the balance, blending a family is far less predictable. There's no perfect recipe and no guaranteed outcomes. Blending a family requires patience, flexibility, and a willingness to embrace the process. It may not always turn out exactly as you envisioned, but with time and care, it can become something truly rich, nourishing, and beautiful.

We'll end where we began by acknowledging the hard truth that building love and embracing a new direction for your blended family is a process of trial and error, layering and blending, stepping back and observing how the flavors interact, and trusting that deeper connections will emerge in time.

~BLENDED FAMILIES 101~
Building a Marriage That Lasts

How can you prioritize quality time together amid the demands of a blended family?

It's easy to get caught up in the daily cycle of childcare, stepparenting, and other schedules. Spending quality time together keeps you stronger, preserves the love, and helps you remember that you are not just parents but lovers. Have date nights regularly, even if it's just an hour a week to reconnect. Treat yourself to weekend getaways without the kids. Design little connection rituals, such as a walk at night or a morning cup of coffee together. Make a commitment to guard this precious time.

How can you maintain open and honest communication, even when discussing difficult topics?

There are often special stressors and points of tension. With communication, you can tackle problems early on, avoid bitterness, and build mutual respect and support. Listen, validate one another's feelings, and be explicit and respectful of what you want. Offer a safe zone for vulnerability and openness. Try setting up check-ins every week or so to talk through any obstacles or issues.

How can you support each other's individual needs and aspirations, even as you navigate the complexities of blended family life?

Maintaining a sense of self in a relationship is vital to a good relationship. Being a champion for each other's own personal growth, interests, and relationships is a way to avoid bitterness and feel fulfilled. Support one another's interests and leave room for your own. Reward each other's successes and provide reassurance in times of hardship. Keep in mind that taking care of yourself makes you a stronger partner.

How can you effectively manage the top three marriage stressors—money, sex, and in-laws—to maintain a healthy and satisfying connection?

These stressors must be well-managed to avoid resentment, conflict, and eventually, the breakup of the marriage, all of which lead to disastrous consequences for children. Discuss money issues openly, draw up a budget together, and work out imbalances. Put intimacy first, even when you have a hectic life, and express what you want and need. Set boundaries with extended family so they don't interfere, and use caution when inviting family and friends into these intimate areas of your marriage. Be open to counseling, attending marriage conferences, or seeking advice from a trusted couple to help work through the issues.

NOTES

Introduction: A Recipe for Success

1. "Six Family Types and Their Unique Dynamics." (2024) *Better Help*. Retrieved from www.betterhelp.com/advice/family/there-are-6-different-family-types-and-each-one-has-a-unique-family-dynamic
2. "Four-in-Ten Couples Are Saying 'I Do, Again.'" Pew Research Center, Washington, D.C. (November 14, 2014). Retrieved from www.pewresearch.org/social-trends/2014/11/14/four-in-ten-couples-are-saying-i-do-again
3. Blended Family. (2024) *Cambridge Dictionary*. Retrieved from https://dictionary.cambridge.org/us/dictionary/english/blended-family
4. McCarthy. K. (2021) "Blended Family Statistics: A Deeper Look Into the Structure." www.lovetoknow.com/parenting/parenthood/blended-family-statistics
5. "Marriage, Family, and Stepfamily Statistics." Retrieved from www.smartstepfamilies.com/smart-help/marriage-family-stepfamily-statistics
6. Chapman, G. and Deal, R. (2020) *Building Love Together in Blended Families: The 5 Love Languages and Becoming Stepfamily Smart.* Chicago, Northfield Publishing.

Chapter 1: Before the Two Become One

1. "5 Risks for People Marrying a Second or Third Time." (2024) *Psychology Today*. Retrieved from www.psychologytoday.com/us/blog/fixing-families/202401/5-dangers-and-opportunities-for-second-and-third-marriages
2. Waldman, L. "Five Reasons Why Second Marriages Might Fail at a High Rate." (2024) *National Register of Health Service Psychologists*. Retrieved from www.findapsychologist.org/five-reasons-why-second-marriages-might-fail-at-a-high-rate-by-dr-larry-waldman

Chapter 2: Dealing with Emotional Adjustments

1. Deal, R. (2014) *The Smart Stepfamily: Seven Steps to a Healthy Family.* Revised and expanded edition. Bloomington, MN: Bethany House Publisher.

Chapter 3: Building Trust and Relationships

1. Small World Solutions Group. (2021) "Superstar Michael Jordan Needed an Assist: Top Teamwork Tips From the Championship Bulls." *Medium*. Retrieved from https://j-brucestewartphd.medium.com/superstar-michael-jordan-needed-an-assist-top-teamwork-tips-from-the-championship-bulls-3a1f-04abb030
2. Tracee White, personal communication through questions from the author, Dec. 2024.

Chapter 4: Managing Different Parenting Styles

1. Segal, J., and Robinson, L. "Blended Family and Step-Parenting Tips." HelpGuide.org.
Retrieved from www.helpguide.org/family/parenting/step-parenting-blended-families
2. Deal, R. (2014) *The Smart Stepfamily: Seven Steps to a Healthy Family.* Revised and expanded edition. Bloomington, MN: Bethany House Publisher.
3. Debowska, A., Hales, G., and Boduszek, D. "Violence Against Children by Stepparents." *The SAGE Handbook of Domestic Violence.* Retrieved from https://pure.hud.ac.uk/files/20139792/Violence_against_children_by_stepparents_Chapter_FINAL.pdf

Chapter 5: Co-Parenting and Coping with Ex-Partners

1. Vellejo, M. (2024) "What Is Co-Parenting? Types, Pros & Cons, and Tips." *Mental Health Center Kids.* Retrieved from https://mentalhealthcenterkids.com/blogs/articles/what-is-co-parenting#:~:text=There%20are%20three%20major%20types,parenting%20style%20for%20any%20family

1. Payne, L. (2023) *S.P.I.L.L—Single Parents Inspiring Love and Legacy.* Updated edition. Thoughts and Theory Publishing.
2. Tracee White, personal communication through questions from the author, Dec. 2024.
3. Etoya White, personal communication through questions from the author, Dec. 2024.

Chapter 6: Adulting: They May Be Grown, But They're Not Gone

1. Deal, R. (2009) "Second-Half Stepfamilies." *Family Life.* Retrieved from www.familylife.com/articles/topics/blended-family/stepparents/developing-a-relationship-with-stepchildren/second-half-stepfamilies

ABOUT THE AUTHOR

LATARISS PAYNE is a best-selling author, dynamic speaker, and certified parenting coach empowering families to thrive. A former IT leader at a Fortune 500 company, Latariss now leads Pathsetters, a program that guides families toward deeper connections. Her work blends practical advice with inspiring insights, encouraging single parents and blended families to overcome challenges and embrace the most important gift of raising healthy, caring children. Latariss is passionate about work-life balance and helping women pursue their dreams while nurturing their families. She brings a unique blend of leadership experience, personal development expertise, and family-focused passion to her writing and speaking engagements.

Latariss is married to her husband, Calvin. She was a single mother to her son until he reached adulthood and now has a family of four children and two grandchildren.

www.ingramcontent.com/pod-product-compliance
Lightning Source LLC
Chambersburg PA
CBHW070431010526
44118CB00014B/1991